UNVEILED

A Story of Redemption

CATHERINE E. BROCK

Copyright © 2019 Catherine E. Brock.
Interior Image Credit: J. Bethany Anderson

All rights reserved. No part of this book may be used or reproduced by any means, graphic, electronic, or mechanical, including photocopying, recording, taping or by any information storage retrieval system without the written permission of the author except in the case of brief quotations embodied in critical articles and reviews.

Scripture taken from the New King James Version®. Copyright © 1982 by Thomas Nelson. Used by permission. All rights reserved.

This book is a work of non-fiction. Unless otherwise noted, the author and the publisher make no explicit guarantees as to the accuracy of the information contained in this book and in some cases, names of people and places have been altered to protect their privacy.

WestBow Press books may be ordered through booksellers or by contacting:

WestBow Press
A Division of Thomas Nelson & Zondervan
1663 Liberty Drive
Bloomington, IN 47403
www.westbowpress.com
1 (866) 928-1240

Because of the dynamic nature of the Internet, any web addresses or links contained in this book may have changed since publication and may no longer be valid. The views expressed in this work are solely those of the author and do not necessarily reflect the views of the publisher, and the publisher hereby disclaims any responsibility for them.

Any people depicted in stock imagery provided by Getty Images are models, and such images are being used for illustrative purposes only.
Certain stock imagery © Getty Images.

ISBN: 978-1-9736-4988-5 (sc)
ISBN: 978-1-9736-4989-2 (hc)
ISBN: 978-1-9736-4987-8 (e)

Library of Congress Control Number: 2018915139

Print information available on the last page.

WestBow Press rev. date: 02/14/2019

To my husband and my children,
my greatest treasures on earth.
I am forever grateful that God gave me you.

To my Adonai from Your Songbird ~
I love You with all of my heart, soul, mind and strength.
This is my sacrifice of praise.

"*Unveiled* is a riveting account of God's unending grace, faithfulness, and pursuit of hearts when darkness keeps knocking at the door. Love is never easy, but it's always worth the fight."

—J. Bethany Anderson
Author of *Kiss My Fish: Tales of Chasing God Around the World*
www.jbethanyanderson.com

"Catherine Brock is a gifted communicator and a passionate lover of Jesus. This is her transparent, heartbreaking and inspiring story of a life ripped apart by the lies of the enemy, but brought back together by the love of Jesus!"

—Julie Earl
President/CEO of Crazy About You Ministries (CAYM)
Author of *No More No: Say Yes to God and Let Him Speak, Work and Love Through You*
www.CrazyAboutYou.org

"Any time spent with Catherine will reveal her tenacity, loyalty, and genuine heart. Voices all around us say that we should be driven, but Catherine has chosen to be led. She takes time regularly to be still and hear/follow the leading of the Holy Spirit. This work is a testament to the ceaseless and amazing work of the Divine through a surrendered heart."

—Lali Stanley
CEO/Co-Founder, Shiloh Restored

"A woman of faith, spirit-filled, Prayer Warrior overflowing with HIS JOY! I am blessed to call Catherine my precious friend and Sister in Christ!"

—Patti Davidson
Co-founder, Door of Hope International Ministry
and Bible Study Teacher

"You did it! You've been obedient! God has been faithful! Keep looking for the rainbows, His promises are UNFAILING!"

—Terri Earls
Wife to one, Mom of six, Co-Developer of *Marriage DNA*
Jasonterri.com

"Catherine, when I think of you, I think of 1 Corinthians 15:58 which says, 'Therefore my beloved (sister), be steadfast, immovable, always abounding in the work of the Lord, knowing that in the Lord your labor is not in vain' (ESV). You have exemplified this scripture and will do the same to all who read *Unveiled*. Your heart has always been one considering 'how to stir up one another to love and good works, not neglecting to meet together, as is the habit of some, but encouraging one another…' (Hebrews 10:24-25, ESV). This is you. May our Father be praised and lifted up by your exaltation of Him through this written testimony! I love you, dear Sister!"

—Novelette Collins
Wife, Mother of five young men and one young lady,
Author of *Raising Davids in a Goliath World*

"Nevertheless when one turns to the Lord, the veil is taken away. Now the Lord is the Spirit; and where the Spirit of the Lord is, there is liberty. But we all, with unveiled face, beholding as in a mirror the glory of the Lord, are being transformed into the same image from glory to glory, just as by the Spirit of the Lord."

~ 2 Corinthians 3:16-18

BEGINNINGS

"There is no fear in love; but perfect love casts out fear, because fear involves torment. But he who fears has not been made perfect in love." I John 4:18

"He who is in you is greater than he who is in the world." I John 4:4

As a young girl, taking a nap one day at my great-grandmother's house, I had a dream. I had a lion for a best friend. He was huge and strong, yet soft and gentle. He was the most loving creature I had ever known and absolutely the most powerful all at the same time. When I was with Him, I never wanted to leave His presence. He was my comforter and my strong defender. I laughed with Him and played with Him and sat in His warm embrace all the day long. Nothing could harm me or come against me when I was with my Lion. I was safe, and I was loved. I didn't want to wake up.

I have never forgotten that dream. As an adult growing closer to God, I began to realize that this dream was not something I conjured up on my own. It was given to me as a gift. This Lion represented my Heavenly Father and His perfect love for me. No matter what I would go through in my life to come, He would always be with me. His ever-enveloping embrace would keep me safe when my world would fall apart over and over again.

CHAPTER 1

*"For You formed my inward parts; You covered me in my mother's womb. I will praise You, for I am fearfully and **wonderfully made; marvelous are Your works,** and that my soul knows very well. My frame was not hidden from You, when I was made in secret, and skillfully wrought in the lowest parts of the earth. Your eyes saw my substance being yet unformed. And in Your book they were all written, the days fashioned for me, when as yet there were none of them."*

~ Psalm 139:13-16

It wasn't always this easy.

I was born December 22, 1969 in Dallas, Texas. My mama was so excited she could have burst. I have pictures of her in her hospital bed, addressing thank-you cards. Alone. Hair pinned perfectly back in a French twist, makeup flawless, like an elegant queen poised to receive guests. My dad left us eight days later.

Fresh from Vietnam, and still fighting his own personal war inside his head, my dad gave up before he started. Running. Scared out of his mind. Fighting for his life.

No doubt Mama was scared too—she just didn't have time to show it then. Immediately attended by her parents, best friends, and my aunt, Mama went into instant protection mode. She was the ultimate nurturer.

Six months later my dad had another family, and Mama and I were left to fend for ourselves. I did see my father and his family on some weekends for the next seven years while Mama and I were still living in Dallas.

Someone even decided it was a good idea that my dad's new wife become my babysitter while my mom went back to work. Unfortunately, I had a habit of biting her daughter.

What I didn't know then was that my mom had attempted suicide shortly after marrying my dad. Dad, an alcoholic among other issues, was providentially sent home from the war after being shot in the foot. They dated just a few short months before being married, apparently deciding this was the next best step in their torrid love affair. Ironically, he was the man who led her to Christ. And then, when I was three, Mama led me to Jesus. I would learn later that I was the only thought that kept her alive when future suicidal thoughts occurred. Jesus and Me. He was her lifeblood.

Mama made the best out of everything. We lived in a cute little yellow two-bedroom house near White Rock Lake and close to my Grandpa and Granny, my dad's father and mother. We had two collies—a sable and white named Winston Churchill and a tri-color named Lady Clementine. Winston was a present from my mom to my dad when they were married, and Clemmie was a present from my dad to my mom. Because my birthday was three days before Christmas, Mama gave me a half-birthday party every summer in June. With a cake and presents and all of my friends. She did not know mediocre. She designed my red and white baby bedroom, painting the red knobs on my white dresser by hand, and topping it off with my giant red and white clown who sat in the white rocker with the red cushion. She sometimes bought me clothes from Neiman Marcus, even though she didn't make much money. I wore white panties with ruffles and eyelet embroidery and got nightgowns for Easter and Valentine's Day. God provided us with everything we needed, and lots of what we wanted.

At home on our own, we had a ball. Once, Mama cut my hair in a bowl cut in the middle of the kitchen floor with instructions from a newspaper article, probably "Hints from Heloise."[1] We habitually listened to Carole King's *Tapestry* album, singing "It's Too Late"[2] as we were rushing around, running late to work and school. Mama and I enjoyed posting up in the den on Thursday nights and watching *The Waltons*[3] on our black-and-white TV and eating her delicious salmon croquettes or ground beef and mixed veggies. On Saturday mornings, I would sit in the den and watch *Sesame Street*[4] or *The Electric Company*[5] and eat fruit-on-the-bottom yogurts. Our den had dark-wood paneling with windows looking out over our huge (at least to me) backyard. Our backyard boasted giant Pecan and Cottonwood trees, and lots and lots of shade. In the spring and summer, we ate pecans from those trees, and the cotton balls from the Cottonwoods would float down and cover our yard like a soft fleece blanket. It was heavenly, and there was no place else I would rather have been. I made secret forts in the back left corner of the yard by the chain-link fence. There was a hole back there that you could crawl through which led to a little run covered with vines that was just big enough for a 6-year old. Time seemed to stop when I was playing pretend. Our home was our safe haven, and it seemed no one could ever take those days from us. We were an inseparable pair.

We had loads of close friends, many of them long-time family friends, because Mama *was* a good friend. She was loyal as the day is long. God graciously placed us next-door to some Christian neighbors who cared for me every day after school. They were an incredibly close family of eight. I knew and loved all of their six children. Their youngest daughter would lay on the floor and prop me upside down on her feet, with my long sandy-blond hair hanging in her face, and call me "Cousin It." God also gave us a serviceman who worked at the Texaco and always fixed "Betsy" (our white Ford sedan with red leather seats) with integrity and without ever over-charging us. Mama called him our guardian angel. Regularly, Mama's Monopoly friends from Texas Employment Commission would come over on a weeknight. We'd all eat dinner and then see who could take over the town. One night, Mama and I came home to a completely wallpapered living room, decked out in the red and blue floral she had previously chosen but hadn't put up yet, compliments of those same friends. On some weekends we would drive down to Salado to the Stage Coach Inn and meet Mama's best friend and her daughter, also on their own without a husband and father. In the summers, we often drove to Galveston or Corpus Christi to hang at the beach with those same friends. Through them, God led Mama and I to a very sound Bible church, Northwest Bible, where we had potluck dinners on Wednesday nights and were regularly fed the Word of God. God surely surrounded us with His love and protection at every turn.

Mama got re-married when I was 6 ½ years old to a man some of our family friends introduced her to, and we moved to Waco six months later. She and I had prayed every night for a husband and a daddy as long as I could remember, so one can imagine my excitement when God finally said, ***"Yes."*** I was even my mom's maid of honor. The wedding was officiated by two reverends, who were the heads of two families who were some of our closest friends. Mama's friends couldn't have been happier for her—everyone was buzzing with joy. My mom and her new husband set out for their honeymoon that day and returned in a few days to start our new lives together. But it wouldn't be long before I would wake up to a new reality that I couldn't comprehend. Everything as I knew it was about to change.

Within six months, my new stepfather had adopted me, and moved us from Dallas to Waco to start a new job. My dad had apparently agreed to the adoption and also to have minimal involvement in my life, so that the three of us could all start our new lives together. We bought a large 2-story early 1900's fixer-upper in the historic district of Waco, across the street from the church we would soon attend. Thankfully Mama and I had family in Waco, and they also attended the same church. I started a new school, which was just two blocks down the street. I made friends rather quickly, but when I came home asking the meaning of certain profane words, my parents began looking into Christian schools. I began 3rd grade at a Christian school, and had to make new friends all over again. My cousins also enrolled shortly after, so there were some familiar faces. But as I remember, I had a little tougher time making friends right away at my new school.

My mama became pregnant rather quickly after she was re-married, and when I was eight years old, my brother was born. I was excited to meet this new bundle of joy, and had been anticipating his arrival greatly. I loved him right away, but soon jealousy set in. I wasn't handling all of the changes well, and soon my world began crashing down around me. And crashing down around my mama. What I remember for the rest of our time in Waco, shortly after my brother was born, was Mama in her room sleeping all day long with her curtains closed. Bipolar depression enveloped her then and didn't fully release its grip on her until she went home to be with Jesus seventeen years later, though she was aided by better medicines in her later years.

We moved to San Antonio when I was in 6th grade. I attended a Christian school there as well, but my world was getting darker and darker. Thankfully, I was surrounded by mainly strong Christian friends and godly families, but even then, I somehow managed to find the outliers of the bunch. Something in me was seeking solace in others who didn't seem to "fit in."

My teenage years were roughly a blur. When I was in eighth grade, we moved to the then very small town of Aledo which boasted a population of a little over 1,100. I began attending public school for the first time since 2nd grade. Almost immediately, I began hanging out with the wrong crowd, and sneaking out, lying to parents, smoking, drinking, drugs and promiscuity were soon to follow. I was a train wreck. My mama continued in her manic depression, with prescription drugs to cope. And it is sufficient to say that my stepfather and I definitely did not have the relationship I was hoping for when I was growing up. In all of this, I often took my frustrations out on my younger brother. Looking back, I have always regretted not being there for him, and basically ignoring him the way that I did in our younger years. He needed help too. I just didn't know how to give it.

I somehow graduated high school being ranked a member of the National Honor Society, despite all the drugs and insanity I was partaking in. Let's just say I was a bit of an over-achiever, at least in the façade I was running. I thought I was doing a pretty good job of fooling everyone, including myself. My friends and I began going to nightclubs in Dallas when I was 16 and a sophomore in high school. I was living the life of Riley. I moved out when I was 18, right after high school, when my best friend's mom moved to Michigan with her boyfriend. My friend had asked me to come live with her in her apartment, which I decided was a supreme idea. I went to a junior college for two years before beginning TCU, all the while continuing my masquerade. My grades were great, so no one noticed how far down the rabbit hole I actually was.

Halfway through college I met a man who was on a similar trajectory. He was easy on the eyes and said he was a Christian, same as me. What?! Did that sound insane to anyone else? Even writing it, I feel bizarre. But it felt completely healthy and normal to me (in my Alice-in-Wonderland truth at the time) to still consider myself a Christian and yet be living the most prodigal life imaginable. I guess because I never shot anything into my body, I considered myself to have standards. Meanwhile, I had probably taken every other recreational drug available up to that point.

Nonetheless, here I was in my distorted reality. Probably very similar to when my mama met my daddy—when I met this man, it was love at first sight.

My new boyfriend seemed to save me from myself, at least for a time. This new man gave me some permanence and stability. At least I could pretend I was doing things the right way, because I was doing them all with the same person. I wasn't as sad as I was before—or was I? A few months into this new relationship, I got a wake-up call. I distinctly remember—upon moving from my apartment where I was living with my best friend, to another place about an hour away with a new roommate—that a deep and dark depression set in all too quickly. And it was truly all too familiar. I found I couldn't be away from this new man for any length of time without crying uncontrollably and being chased constantly by overwhelming fear. I found it hard to function normally. I even tried to start a new job and was unsuccessful because I was always crying. The hole in my soul was growing deeper. Terrified of being alone, I filled the hole by moving near my boyfriend. Little did I know the bottom was about to drop out.

In my junior year in college, shortly after taking my last final, I went to the hospital to see my mama, who was having a hysterectomy. I was greeted in the gift shop by my stepfather's friend, who decided it was his duty to tell me why my mom was really there. As the word "cancer" tumbled out of his mouth like vomit, the room started to spin. How could this be true? How could she have kept this from me? Dismissing this inappropriate revelation, I got to my mom in her hospital room as quickly as I could. Upon hearing my question, she confirmed the disastrous news. My world was spiraling out of control.

CHAPTER 2

"Beloved, do not think it strange concerning the fiery trial which is to try you, as though some strange thing happened to you; but rejoice to the extent that you partake of Christ's sufferings, that when His glory is revealed, you may also be glad with exceeding joy."

~ 1 Peter 4:12-13

Five years after beginning college, I graduated from TCU and was engaged to marry my boyfriend. I graduated Magna Cum Laude, despite doing recreational drugs all the way through college. My façade was working, or so I thought. No one could see my cavern was turning into a black hole.

Marriage just seemed like my salvation. Surely this man could save me from myself, now that my rock was dying. Little did I know that I was in for more surprises. Three weeks before we were to be married, I was hit by another bombshell. While hanging with friends at our favorite bar one night when my fiancé was away on business, my girlfriend pulled me out to the car to reveal to me that my fiancé had been cheating on me for at least one year. Upon confronting him, I discovered the validity of this accusation, even though he only admitted to about half of the truth. I was mortified. I called my mama. I called his mama. Both mothers came to my apartment to have an intervention. They loved us and just wanted things to work out between us. And secretly, I think my mama wanted to make sure I was taken care of, now that she knew she was dying. Both women were intent on counseling us to stay together. But this was an extreme wake-up call. And instead of heeding the warning before me and leaning on my Lord, I succumbed to the fear of being alone, and to pressure of what others would think of me in this calamitous state. I got married three weeks later.

Our marriage began with a rocky start, to say the least. And there seemed to be no end in sight. Neither my new husband nor I were turning to the Lord. Our masquerade grew bigger and sicker. We continued living for ourselves, buying things on credit that we couldn't afford, driving cars we could barely afford, and drinking and doing drugs with our friends on the weekends, and even during the week. We partied and lived selfishly and listened to music that supported all that we lived for. We had no thought but for the moment and for ourselves. During that hurricane season, I learned that my new husband struggled with some of his own addictions that threatened our marriage. We were living fast and furiously and not slowing down to accept the consequences. But they were coming.

In October of 1995, I got a phone call from my stepfather. My mother was going on hospice. Time to wake up. I shared my circumstances with my bosses at Neiman Marcus, and they told me to go to her, assuring me I would have a job when I was ready to return. I could no longer ignore the truth. What had been looming before me and threatening to steal my very air was now breathing down my neck. Life was coming to a screeching halt.

I spent the next days and weeks by my mom's side most every day and many nights. For much of that time it was just the two of us, as my stepdad was working out of town most of the week days. The days were long, but not long enough. And the nights were even longer. It is really a scary thing being alone in the middle of the night with someone you love so dearly who is dying. It feels like the earth could just swallow you up at any given second. Depression so easily sets in when your guard is down. I began to lose weight quickly. Mama wasn't eating, and I didn't want to eat either. I kept returning to the grocery store for new and better flavors of Ensure to try and feed her starving body. I remember being so frustrated that she wouldn't even try it. She knew she was dying. She was ready to see Jesus face to face. I just wasn't ready for her to go.

Meanwhile, back at home with my husband, things were rapidly on the decline. He had agreed to my quitting my job to be with my mom, but was obviously feeling neglected. He began complaining about simple housework not being done and about his needs not being met. On one particular day, he emphatically remarked that he had a cold and that I didn't even care. Sadly, at this point in both our young and extremely immature lives, all of these things were true, and I couldn't have cared less about fixing any one of them. We had been living so egotistically and in a continual pattern of hurting each other for our own selfish gain, sweeping every hurt feeling and wound to our souls right under that perpetual rug. What was one more? I blatantly blurted out that I didn't care about his cold when my mom was dying of cancer, and that he could definitely do his own laundry, that he was a big boy. We were falling apart at the seams.

Enter the enemy. 1 Peter 5:8 warns, "Be sober, be vigilant; because your adversary the devil walks about like a roaring lion, seeking whom he may devour." My husband and I were back-sliding believers, Christians in name only, and were definitely nowhere close to being sober or vigilant. We were anything but. Satan knew that, and as he studied us, knew exactly when and where to pounce. One Saturday when my husband was working, I was home taking a much-needed mental break from deathwatch at my mama's house. I received a phone call from a male friend whom I knew from my restaurant days in college. He hung out with my husband and I and our group of friends quite frequently, so this was not abnormal. He invited me to come hang out with him that morning. I went. Alone. Going to another man's house without my husband should have already been off limits. But we were living foolishly, never thinking about consequences. Subconsciously, I was probably looking for an escape. The disguise looked benign enough, and I took the bait. I remember driving home that afternoon, considering having an affair. The thoughts kept dangerously pushing their way into the exterior of my mind. They were so pleasure-inducing that I ignored the danger and entertained them all the way home.

A week or so later, the enemy got his chance. My male friend called again one Saturday, this time asking me to come hang out with him at Frye Street Fair in Denton. My husband already had other plans with his best friend, so I made the choice to go with my friend. The day was a whirlwind of drugs, alcohol, music, food, and flirting. It ended with me committing adultery.

Now my world was spinning out of control. My mom was dying. My marriage was going to Hades in a handbasket. And I had just betrayed my husband and God, not to mention putting my friendship in a horribly awkward state. There was no turning back. But at that moment, I didn't even want to. My heart began telling me crazy lies and distorting the truth completely. All of a sudden, my world went from complete despair and a reality of death that I couldn't process, to an ecstasy of something—someone—to look forward to daily. It was an enigma. It was a crazy rush. I needed it and craved it. It became my new addiction.

Simultaneously, I was already forming some other addictions. When Mama originally went on hospice, I had asked my gynecologist to prescribe Valium for me, at a co-worker's suggestion. Mom had ovarian cancer, and this doctor was treating her as well, so he understood my pain. The doctor had obliged my Valium request then. In a few short weeks, when that didn't seem to be doing the trick, the "helpful" co-worker suggested Xanax. I then asked the doctor to change my prescription to this more intense drug, and he obliged. Then, when I told the doctor I needed him to increase my dosage, he obliged again. When I later told him I needed an antidepressant, he prescribed it. I was escaping my pain at every turn possible, never dreaming I was gouging out my soul with my eyes wide open.

On Thanksgiving Day, 1995 as my mama lay dying, relatives and friends were piling in. In a last-ditch effort to escape every madness that lay before me, I got in my car and drove to a restaurant/bar to meet my boyfriend. In my oblivion, the stupidity of that dichotomy never crossed my mind. I couldn't process the pain I was running from, so I focused on the freedom I thought I was running to. I couldn't have been more wrong, but no one could tell me anything. I was actually confronted about the adultery on that very same day by my uncle, and later by my aunt, who incidentally are divorced and cornered me separately. Both conversations happened before I left for the bar. But it didn't matter. My mind was made up. I was running straight for the looney bin.

By the time I returned from my diversion that evening, Mama had departed this old world to live eternally with Jesus in heaven. I just remember parking my car in front of their house. My husband greeted me there. He told me she was gone. I think I dropped my keys somewhere in the front yard and ran inside. My father and stepmother were there, along with my grandmother (Mama's mom), aunt and stepdad. I would learn later that my aunt and stepmom were praying with her when she passed. But what I witnessed that day, in my overwhelming grief, was a joyous miracle no one can or ever will take from me. My mama's body lay before me, her face with rosy cheeks and a smile to beat the band. Her youthful glow was other-worldly. The sallow, yellow, morphine-induced, eyes-rolled–back-in-her-head countenance had changed the instant my mama saw the face of Jesus. She was not here anymore. She was clearly sitting at Jesus' feet. The witnesses, my dad and my stepmom, would later tell me the story of watching Mama take her last breath, and *then* the smile and rosy glow appearing. They knew it was miraculous, and didn't want me to miss this all-important fact about my mama's passing.

Nevertheless, I kept running. I ran for the next three and a half years. A few days later, on the night before my mama's funeral, I told my husband about the affair I had been having. It had been happening just about one month by that time, and the lying I was doing was like a pressure-cooker to my soul. I felt like I would explode from all of the pain and sin. So, I dug in deeper. I created an even wider gap between the man I loved and myself, and myself and God. I remember telling my husband my secret while sitting at a loud, crowded Uptown Dallas restaurant across the table from two of our best friends. Our poor friends were caught in a quagmire. But in my self-absorbed state, I didn't care. I wanted everyone to hurt as much as I was hurting. And hurt them I did. All of them. The manner in which I told my husband of all my lying and the affair was hateful and mean. And it didn't stop there. That night, when my husband and I were alone, I told him that I never loved him and I shouldn't have married him and that I wanted a divorce—instantly. Needless to say, he was bewildered. He was never mean or rude, though. He was just sad and hurt. I had accomplished my purpose. I was wrecking everything in my path.

By this time, and actually since I was a little girl, my father had been walking with God, and was sold out to Jesus. I moved in with his family and lived there off and on as I was trying to find my way. That year was a complete blur. Just a blip I would love to forget for the rest of my life. I was 97 pounds with bleached-blond hair and a vendetta. I was on a mission to ruin every good thing in my life. Thankfully, during this time I did quit taking the prescription drugs. Because I grew up seeing my mama's dependence on prescription drugs, I was afraid to get stuck in the same rut. Amazing how I could rationalize some crazy things in my life while putting the kibosh on others. I went back to my job, and within a few months, I had moved out of my father's house and into an apartment in Dallas—with a roommate I met in the apartment office as I was filling out the lease application. I would soon learn that my new roommate was anorexic and bulimic—the two of us did <u>not</u> make a healthy pair. I continued in my on-again, off-again affair with the man. When we were off, I saw my husband a few times and tried to make a last-ditch effort at saving my marriage—not a whole-hearted effort, I might add. I dated around a little and basically just tried to pretend I wasn't crazy.

In April of 1996, my divorce was final. I remember walking in to the courtroom and feeling the weight of the world on my shoulders. When I met my attorney, and saw the look on her face as she saw *my* expression, I began to cry. She reminded me that I didn't have to go through with the divorce, that I could choose to back out and turn it all around. But I was too deep in. I was not walking with the Lord, and didn't have what it took to make that difficult decision at that time. I shook my head and said no, I was going through with what I started. I sealed my fate and ended my marriage in that courtroom for good. What a terribly sad day that was.

To ease my pain, I just kept going on in my disaster-making, ignoring warning signs and trying to forget all of the destruction I had caused, pretending like everything was ok. I left the job at Neiman's, and was hired as a showroom manager at a wholesale apparel showroom in the International Apparel Mart of Dallas. Soon after, I moved out of the apartment where I lived with my roommate, and into my own apartment. Finally, in an "on-again" time with the man I left my husband for, when my self-esteem could not go any lower, I asked God to help me break up with the boyfriend for good. He did. I said goodbye to the man in December of 1996, in a bar, on my birthday, after begging him to decide to see only me, as he had now expressed his desire to see other people while still seeing me. Thankfully, that was what it took for me to pick myself up off the floor and declare this mosh-pit dance officially over. Funny how sin begets sin. You wind up saying yes to things you always disdained before. The more times you let your guard down and compromise with the devil, the bigger bite he takes out of your soul.

CHAPTER 3

"But the very hairs of your head are all numbered. Do not fear therefore; you are of more value than many sparrows."

~ Luke 12:7

Lonely, scared to death, and looking for a way out, I contemplated suicide more than once. I remember driving over a downtown Dallas bridge in the dark early morning on my way to work one day, imagining through my tears that with just one flick of the wrist I would be over the guardrail and plunging to my death, but free from all of this pain. Something always kept me from taking my own life, though. Fear of the Lord, maybe. Maybe just plain fear.

One night in April 1997, alone with my dog in my new apartment, I cried out to God. I was weeping and on the floor. I told Him how desperate I was. I told Him I knew by now that a man was not my answer, but that I needed Him to please rescue me. Right then I had a vision. I had never had a vision before then; but this did not make me feel fearful. In fact, it brought me joy. I saw in my mind a man I knew through mutual friends, but had not seen for at least a year. I even knew where he worked, because my friend worked at the same restaurant. At that moment, I actually picked up the phone and dialed the number to the restaurant, hanging up hurriedly when I realized the foolishness of that decision.

The next evening, a friend came to rescue me from my sad state. We went to a place where we could be around other people and have a little fun. Within 30 minutes, this man from my vision the night before walked into the place. I don't know how to describe the feeling I had when I saw him, except to say I had peace. He was very happy to see me, and he picked me up off the floor and swung me around, asking where I had been all of this time. Within minutes, he was sitting at our table. We never stopped looking into each other's eyes the entire night. Our conversation was so comfortable—like we had known each other our whole lives. When the place closed, we took our friends home, and then just stood in the parking lot talking for a very long time. He asked for my number, and eventually we hugged and said goodbye. He called me the very next day. We dated for the next four years.

I wish I could say that I honored God in this relationship, especially since I truly believe this was a gift straight from Him. But sadly, I did not. Our relationship began like everything else in my life seemed to—backwards. I often wonder what treasure God had in store for me, had I kept His commands for my life to the utmost.

In October of 1997, my new boyfriend and I moved to New York City. I left the Dallas showroom job, and was quickly hired as the Dallas sales representative for a sweater manufacturer in the NY garment district. I was making twice as much money as I had made in Dallas, and thought I was on top of the world. My new boyfriend was a stock market day trader when we lived in Dallas, and had now taken a day-trading job at a firm on Long Island. We drove for three days to our new home, our car packed to the gills with our dog and our worldly possessions, hauling a U-haul trailer behind us with the rest. On our third day of driving, as we arrived in Virginia, my boyfriend called his new bosses to check in. They immediately informed him that due to the stock market crash that had happened that morning, they had just lost half the money they had set aside for him to trade. They told him he would be working from this vantage point, beginning with a thousands-in-the-hole deficit. We took the news on the chin and carried on, not realizing the foreshadowing of this major event. Young and dumb seemed to characterize both of us in those days.

We lived in the city for three months before finding an apartment of our own at a nice high-rise in New Jersey, just across the Hudson River. We thought this would be a great adventure, and at first it was just that. Everything was new and exciting (including the weather!), and there were practically surprises at every turn. The people were interesting and very different from what we were accustomed to at home in the DFW Metroplex. There was wonderful food on every corner, new sights to see every day, and great fun to be had on the weekends.

But the fun eventually wore off. It wasn't long before I realized I really hated my new job. My bosses, and the company I worked for, were not as wonderful as they seemed when I interviewed with them at the Dallas market. I cried to my boyfriend many nights when he picked me up from work in the city, as I recounted yet another ruinous day in the world of fashion. Besides trading stocks during the day, he waited tables in the afternoons and evenings so we could make ends meet. We hardly ever saw each other, and we barely had any money. What little we did have, we usually ended up spending foolishly going to clubs or out with friends who were spontaneously visiting us on the weekends. After two and a half months, I was fired from my new job because the wife, of the husband-and-wife team I worked for, had it in for me. I cried and then laughed when I saw my boyfriend that afternoon, so glad to be free from the daily torture I was enduring.

Thankfully, God had so much mercy on us, even while we were out of His will. I got another job within three weeks working for a coat manufacturer, making considerably less than I was making at the sweater company, but I didn't care. I was the Dallas rep for this company as well, and still got to stay with my family when I went home every few months for markets. During this time, I was sued by the previous company I worked for because of an unemployment issue. The hits just kept on coming. My current boss was called to testify in the court mediation. Following this event, she even remarked to a salesperson in our showroom that it was obvious this couple had it out for me. The judge said I was guilty of the charge and then ordered my fine—$0.00! Again, God's complete mercy when I did not deserve it. I had been working at the coat company for six months, when an old friend called me. I knew her from the Dallas company I was working for before we moved, and she had recently opened her own showroom. She apprised me of a national sales manager position opening with the suit manufacturer she currently represented. I applied immediately and got the job. They increased my pay by a little, but not much to speak of. There was more freedom in this job, however. I ran the whole New York showroom and worked with key accounts there, besides still getting to travel home to Dallas for markets, and also to California and to stores in the Northeast. The owners were Christians, so it felt more like home to me. Even though I still wasn't really walking with God, He never stopped loving me and being gracious to me. He was slowly bringing me back to Himself all along the way.

Over the next several months, I began praying more and reading my Bible. Grandpa had given me a One-Year Bible, and this made it easy for me to spend a little time every day delving into the Old and New Testaments. I called my dad many times during this searching phase and conveyed difficulties in my job and in my relationship with my boyfriend, and just life in general. He always had one answer for me. "Run to Jesus," he would reply. When I asked him what he meant by that, he never elaborated. I soon began desiring to hear more of the Word of God. I perused the television channels available to people without cable and did not find much church on TV. The Northeast is not typically known for its religious outpourings, at least not like the Bible belt of Texas is. You can't just find church on any channel on a Sunday. My boyfriend and I began talking about going to church, and we soon found a little Baptist church in Hoboken and began attending.

During this time, I was starting to feel an uneasiness about my physical relationship with my boyfriend. I turned to my Bible to find answers that would hopefully untie the knot in my stomach. God is very clear in His Word about the issue of premarital sex (Hebrews 13:4, 1 Corinthians 6:13, I Corinthians 7:2, Ephesians 5:3, Genesis 2:24, I Corinthians 6:18). But even with all of this evidence, I tried to rationalize my lifestyle with God. I often asked God what He meant by what He said about sex and marriage, and attempted to justify my situation by assessing us as "common-law married." That wasn't cutting it, though. The check in my spirit would not subside. I became more and more uneasy as we continued in our lifestyle, which was clearly contradictory to the truth I was reading in God's Word. Eventually I became so uneasy about the issue that I asked my boyfriend to sit down and discuss it with me. Once we did, I told him I was no longer comfortable with our physical intimacy, outside of marriage. He didn't fully understand this newfound attempt at chastity, but did agree to comply and didn't give me any grief over it. In fact, he was very loving and accepting of me, even in this seemingly strange turn in our relationship.

Eventually we were engaged, but our relationship became more and more tumultuous as we continued to live together—instead of separately until we were married.

One morning at the beginning of June 1999, around 6 a.m., I was immediately awakened by a frightening, yet awesome sound of swirling wind and whispering that filled the room. To this day, I cannot explain what the Voice was saying, only that it engulfed me and terrified me so that I sat straight up in my bed. The sound stopped as abruptly as it had started. I shook my fiancé to wake him and inquire what he had heard. Nothing. The Voice was just for me. Terrified, I shot out of bed and curled up in my big red chair in the living room with my Bible. Ironically, this book was the only thing bringing me comfort at that moment. Almost afraid to know the answer, I asked God, "Please tell me what You are saying to me; please show me what You want me to see." I opened my Bible directly to Isaiah 43. Verses 1-3 seemed to leap off the page at me that morning. God said to me in that passage, "But now, thus says the LORD, who created you, O Jacob, and He who formed you, O Israel: Fear not, for I have redeemed you. I have called *you* by your name; you *are* mine. When you walk through the waters, I *will be* with you; and through the rivers, they shall not overflow you. When you walk through the fire you shall not be burned, nor shall the flame scorch you. For I *am* the LORD your God, the Holy One of Israel, your Savior." The passage goes on to describe how God gave nations for me, for my ransom, because I was precious in His sight and because I have been honored and He has loved me. It talks on and on about giving men for me and people for my life and how He would bring my descendants from the east and gather us from the west, and that I was not to fear because He is with me. It is a glorious redemption story of God bringing back His own from the ends of the earth, because we who are His have been created for His glory. It is truly a love story. And it was just for me.

From that point on, I felt I had my marching orders from the Almighty. The passage in Isaiah referenced coming out of Babylon. That day I understood God to mean the New York/New Jersey area where I was living and working, and that I was to go home—to "run to Jesus." For once in my life I wanted to do something right. I knew I needed to obey God, and that the rest would follow. The instructions, the specifics, the financial provision, all of it. Eventually I broke the news to my fiancé and began making preparations to move home to Dallas. I don't know if he really understood at that point—it may have been pretty confusing to him. I can't say I understood it all either, except to say that I knew I had to obey the Lord. I knew in my heart this was the right thing to do, even though parts of it felt messy. But God began working out the details, one by one, affirming my decision to obey. I called my dad and asked if I could come and live with them. The answer was an immediate "yes." I made a plane reservation for three weeks out because of the cost, but this gave me time to tie up loose ends. I sat down with my bosses, who were so understanding it was almost scary, and they offered to pay for my move home. This was just further confirmation that I was following the Holy Spirit. My Christian employers knew that I had been living out of God's will, and that this was a definite step in the right direction. They set such an example to me then as Christians by encouraging me in my faith walk, even though I was leaving them without a national salesperson. I also called my boss at the showroom I left in Dallas to ask for my old job back. He agreed, and increased my salary by $15k, given my current New York experience in the industry. Another big pat on the back from God. My fiancé and I agreed that I would take our only car with me, since public transportation was much more readily available in the Northeast, and I arranged to have the car brought back to Dallas. This part was not quite as simple. My car took seven months to arrive home because of complications with the company. But to me, this was a small price to pay for the peace I felt in finally obeying my Heavenly Father. There are often costs associated with obedience, as well as costs associated with disobedience. This seemed to be some of both. Regardless, I felt relief and joy and the Lord's arms around me constantly. I knew my heart had peace with Jesus.

The next few months were a little messy to say the least. I moved back in with my dad and shared a room with my 17-year-old, high-school-senior sister. I shared a car with my family. The familiar job afforded me peace of mind, as well as the opportunity to be back and forth to New York for markets, so I got to see my fiancé some and also bring things home from storage. This also made way for more physical temptation, which was extremely inviting in our now on-again/off-again relationship. I fell several times during this period in my new walk. But finally we made the decision to abstain until marriage, and did so for fourteen months until our wedding. I met some girls at my job in Dallas, fellow showroom managers, and we began going out to clubs and bars together. Eventually, though, my conscience began to hurt from this kind of thing; and even listening to the old music from my not-so-distant past became offensive to the Jesus I now felt living in my heart. It was like a lightbulb was turned on permanently and would not turn off. My flesh constantly pulled at me to fulfill lusts in different habitual areas; but, one by one, these old habits died as my love for Christ grew and became more alive. Now I only wanted to please *Him*. Anything else felt second best. He was my Lord and my King and my Savior. And I couldn't thank Him enough for saving me from myself.

CHAPTER 4

"At my first defense no one stood with me, but all forsook me. May it not be charged against them. But the Lord stood with me and strengthened me, so that the message might be preached fully through me, and that all the Gentiles might hear. Also, I was delivered out of the mouth of the lion."

~ 2 Timothy 4:16-17

By February of 2000 my fiancé had moved home to Texas. That year I also moved out of my father's house and into my own apartment. In September, I quit my job as a showroom manager and launched out in a new venture, opening my own showroom. I called it "Catrinka" after a nickname my mama had for me when I was little. My fiancé and I took a trip back to NYC, where I secured all the new apparel lines I would represent in my showroom. As I stepped into each new appointment during that 10-day trip, owners and manufacturers continued to say "yes" to this green young lady just starting out into the unknown. It was truly miraculous—and looking back, I am forever grateful. God really guided me through this process, giving me one great line which was to be my bread and butter, and several other novelty lines to support my cash flow and provide variety to the room and to buyers.

My new fiancé even surprised me in New York with a beautiful diamond engagement ring, and then a new computer for my business, at a romantic dinner in the city one night during our stay. We arrived back in Dallas with all that we needed to begin my new business. We hit the ground running and the showroom opened the following month, at the

October major spring market. It was a fabulous opening, and we were on cloud nine. We had already begun making wedding plans, and we were married in May of 2001. We moved into a two-bedroom apartment of our own in North Dallas near the tollway. Even now, God's faithfulness to us through all of that time seems so undeserved. He is truly a merciful, gracious, loving and forgiving God—willing and ready to receive all who confess their sins in true repentance to Him.

Our marriage began in a whirlwind. We had no idea what we were doing or the slightest idea of what a successful marriage looked like. Neither of us had grown up with a good model of a godly marriage; we were pretty much winging it. Hmmm, sound familiar? We knew we were happy, young and in love and didn't process much beyond that. We had been to a premarital class at the Fellowship Bible church we were attending. Beyond that, we were clueless. I clearly had some good ideas of what NOT to do at this point, but didn't have much else figured out. I knew I was walking with the Lord now, and that He would guide us. I knew that He had shown my new husband to me, and believed it was His will that we marry. I wanted badly to be pregnant and would sometimes get teary-eyed when I saw pregnant women. My husband and I decided we would wait one year before we started trying. We were pregnant within eight months! God was indeed in control.

In the beginning of my pregnancy, we began looking for a house. We knew we weren't quite ready financially, but we wanted to have some idea of what we were looking for. We looked at only two houses before we found the one we wanted. God quickly put us on the same page about our new home when we walked into it for the first time. We looked no further, but we also knew it would be several months before we were in the position to buy. Neither one of us had ever lived in this kind of house before, and doubt soon sprang up in my mind. I began praying for this home, and immediately heard an all-too-familiar voice that said, "Why would you pray for a house like that? You've never lived anywhere like that before." Almost as immediately, then came a second, strong and peaceful voice. It said, **"Why wouldn't you pray for this house?"** I believed then and there that this was the Holy Spirit. I prayed for the house for eight months.

In October of 2002, we were blessed with our first child, a baby boy. Words could not express our gratitude to our Heavenly Father for this miraculous little creature, a supreme and undeserved blessing from God. He was truly heaven-sent, and we were experiencing more abundance than we could have ever asked or thought.

Unbeknown to me, my husband was continuing to check the status of the house I was praying for and to stay in touch with the Realtor®. When he was financially ready to make our offer, our house was still available and had come down considerably from the original asking price, another huge blessing from God. We moved in to our new home when our baby boy was three months old.

It was not long before bliss turned to strife. Given our combined spiritual immaturity and my fairly recent spiritual transformation, we were a little off balance. I subconsciously decided that it was my duty to lead us spiritually, since I now had this newfound love for Christ and was actively changing my behavior to follow Him. To put it mildly, this was off-putting to my new husband, who didn't grow up going to church or with much dialogue at all about God. I knew from conversations we had while dating that he had asked Jesus to come into his heart as a young child of five years old, being sent away by his mother in the summertime on a bus to a Baptist church. There he had made a profession of faith and had been baptized. He had come home and had told no one, not even his mother and father. I had considered myself a Christian since I was three years old and had attempted to lead us in matters of faith, even when I wasn't walking with Christ. Now that I was, it made sense to me that I would show him the ropes. Surely my new husband would appreciate all of my Biblical knowledge and the ways I was hearing from God! Nothing could have been further from the truth.

When our son was six months old, I sold my business to be a stay-at-home mom. I was so thrilled about my darling boy, and I was struggling to balance my time between him and my business. Looking back, this was another move I should have made a little differently. Not that I would have kept my business. I just wish I understood at the time how to pray and wait on God, as opposed to nagging my husband into the decision I thought we should make. I did pray, but I also nagged. It did not do wonders for my marriage. My husband's family of origin was very different than mine, and he had grown up with his mom always working and paying half the bills. My mom had only worked until she didn't have to, and even with her depression, I had enjoyed the benefits of having her there. Needless to say, I got my way, but not really in the best possible way. I did not realize then that I was continuing to drive a wedge between my husband and me by refusing to come under his leadership for our family.

Thankfully, we had joined a very strong Bible Fellowship church when I was eight months pregnant. We had a very wise and strong pastor who knew God's Word backward and forward. The body was also very closely knit, and had a heavy emphasis on serving. We joined a small group, and became very involved with our new church family. But even with all of this help, our relationship continued to sour. I continued to try to lead us, while not really acknowledging my sin, and my husband grew further from me and further from God. Truthfully, before we knew it, we were both very far from God.

Oh, it seemed I was doing everything right. My house was in order from the outside. I looked the part and acted the part of the perfect wife and mom. I served in ministries, facilitated a Bible study group at the church, signed up to help people in need, attended church three times a week, and on and on. When our son was almost two years old, I gave my testimony in our megachurch on a Wednesday night, my husband standing with me, glorifying God for healing my wrists miraculously from a year and a half of carpal tunnel syndrome and tendonitis, that a hand surgeon told me was incurable without surgery. When our son was two and a half years old, my husband and I even went on a mission trip to South Africa for twelve days, and I led at least ten people to Christ. But little did I know how far apart my marriage was growing from this holy God I was serving.

In September of 2004, the Lord began telling me and teaching me how to fast. I began doing a 24-hour fast weekly at first, and later just fasted as the Lord led me. Little did I know fasting and praying would become my lifeline in the days, months, and years to come. Jesus was teaching me about the fellowship of suffering with Him. He continued to sustain me through His Word and through His promises. All the while our marriage was growing more and more chaotic and strained. By the time our son was two years old, our fighting had erupted to violence, and over the next few years, police involvement would become more and more frequent. My husband was more and more critical, angry and abusive; while I was more and more codependent and tried to fix everything.

The more hurtful he was, the more submissive I thought I needed to be, thinking it must have all been my fault because I wasn't being "godly" enough. Then when I couldn't take any more abuse, like a volcano I would erupt. I began to notice our young son imitating his father's abusive and condescending ways. I was seriously considering separation. I had occasional suicidal thoughts, but because of our son, God's truth always won, bringing me back to sanity and just laying constantly at the Lord's feet. When God wasn't giving me a dream, I frequently had disturbing dreams from the enemy that made me feel depressed, guilty, or angry upon awakening.

Sadly, many times while trying to control my anger toward my husband, I indirectly fired off at our young son. Oh, how I wish I could get those days back! I would do things so differently. And yet, I never want to be there again—not for anything. The Lord was literally my breath, the air in my lungs, every waking minute. I never would have made it through without His saving grace.

I didn't take a step without talking to my heavenly Father now. Not that I was always getting it right, but I took everything to Him in prayer. He was constantly teaching me how to be a godly wife, despite my desperate circumstances. Meanwhile, my husband seemed to be moving further and further away from me—and from God. I kept coming back to the Lord and asking Him how I could do things better and get it right this time. He continued to sustain me and to teach me how to be loving and respectful, even when I was not being loved in return. At night, when my husband was sleeping, I often anointed his head with oil and prayed over him and over our marriage. I knew God was using everything and that He was working, but my journey was slow and painful.

He often gave me the same passages. 2 Corinthians 3:18, Psalm 18, Romans 8:35-39, Romans 8:1 and many, many others. One frequent message from my Father was Proverbs 21:1, "The king's heart is in the hand of the LORD, like the rivers of water; He turns it wherever He wishes." Then He backed that up with, "Better to live on a corner of the roof than share a house with a quarrelsome wife" (Proverbs 21:9). Ouch, but true. Another strengthening verse God often gave me was Joshua 1:9, "Have I not commanded you? Be strong and of good courage; do not be afraid, nor be dismayed, for the LORD you God *is* with you wherever you go."

I was learning about boundaries as well, about how to speak to someone with whom you are in a repeated pattern of abuse and to escape these conversations when necessary, so as not to continue the pattern of abuse. All the while, our young son was hearing all of the fights and taunting and jeering, and had on more than one occasion stood up to his father in my defense. This was not the life I wanted to be leading. I felt like an anomaly, like no one I knew at church or my friends or family could really relate to or understand what I was completely dealing with at home. I knew that God was my Rock, though. Ultimately, I would have lost my sanity without His love and guidance DAILY. He was truly my daily bread.

CHAPTER 5

"Be glad then, you children of Zion, and rejoice in the LORD your God; for He has given you the former rain faithfully, and He will cause the rain to come down for you—the former rain, and the latter rain in the first month. The threshing floors shall be full of wheat, and the vats shall overflow with new wine and oil. So I will restore to you the years that the swarming locust has eaten, the crawling locust, the consuming locust, and the chewing locust, My great army which I sent among you. You shall eat in plenty and by satisfied, and praise the name of the LORD your God, who has dealt wondrously with you; and My people shall never be put to shame. Then you shall know that I am in the midst of Israel: I am the LORD your God and there is no other. My people shall never be put to shame."

~ Joel 2:23-27

One morning in 2005, I awoke from a dream. The words, **"I will repay the years the locust has eaten"** were being repeated over and over in my head. Little did I know the Lord would give me this verse day after day, year after year in our upcoming journey through the valley of the shadow of death. This promise, found in Joel 2:25, would become my mantra in the years to come. About a year later, my husband was awakened in the middle of the night from the same words being spoken to him by the Holy Spirit in his sleep.

I can truly say that the brightest spot of that year 2005 was when our then two-and-a-half-year-old son asked Jesus to come into his heart. He was in the bathtub, and began asking questions about a picture he had colored with the three crosses on it. He asked me why there were three crosses, and I explained that besides Jesus being crucified, two criminals (bad men) were also crucified with him. I then told of how one of the criminals chose to believe in Jesus while they were hanging on their crosses, and Jesus told him that day he would be with Him in paradise (Luke 23:26-43). Our son, bursting with enthusiasm, insisted that he too was going to become part of God's kingdom that day. In my 'mom" way, I tried to postpone his decision a little, until I deemed him old enough to understand. But he was having none of it. No one could stop that boy from becoming Christ's own. Looking back, that story was foreshadowing for his entire life. I would come to learn later that this passion would characterize his very being.

There were many other respites along the way. The Lord knows that we cannot continue in our own strength; and His Word says, "Hope deferred makes the heart sick. But when the desire comes, it is a tree of life" (Proverbs 13:12). I became pregnant again when our son was three, almost four years old. At that point in our marriage, my husband and I were so far apart, it was a miracle we had another child. At the time I became pregnant, I had been praying for over two and a half years for another baby. God heard my prayers and was merciful. The Lord had told me several times (and my husband at least once) over those years that He was going to give us another child. Then, right before I discovered I was pregnant, the Lord prophesied over my womb through one of my best friends; we will call her "Tanya." She would later come to be known as one of my "Soul Sisters." The verse being read aloud in church that night was Psalm 113:9, about the barren woman. Tanya held my tummy and said the Lord led her to pray for me. She began to speak life to my womb, and to ask that in God's timing, He would give us another child. I wept uncontrollably and hugged my friend, thanking her for her obedience.

The next day, the Lord gave me Psalm 115:14-16, which talks about God blessing me with increase more and more, my children and me. Everywhere I looked there were messages about babies—on TV, in devotionals the Lord led me to, in a movie I watched with my husband. The Holy Spirit was clearly speaking His truth over my life once again, illuminating scripture and everything around us. When we discovered I was pregnant, we were both truly overjoyed.

And during that time, I asked God to give my husband our baby's name. He called me one day with a name he liked that would be great for a boy or a girl. I loved it and said yes. When I looked up the name that evening, I learned the Hebraic meaning is "God has heard." I wept and knelt on the floor in praise and admiration of my Savior, the omnipotent God who knows all things.

In January of 2006 I had a dream. I was in an apartment with a small child who was my daughter. A terribly evil red-haired pasty-faced man came in and raped us both. I was crying out to people in the room and in the apartment to help me. There were several of my family members, siblings, there. No one helped us. In fact, they laughed and said they thought it was a joke. I knew then the dream was about Satan trying to destroy my family, and no one believing me—no one coming to my defense. I awoke, once again terrified to start my day. Immediately, when I got in the Word, God poured His love over me. Joel 2:25. Galatians 5:1. 2 Timothy 2:23-24. 2 Timothy 3:1-7. Looking back now, I believe the dream was more specifically a threat to me from the enemy about my daughter. Discerning from the date written in my journal, I believe that dream actually occurred on the night she was conceived. God would surely show me over the years to follow that my daughter and I, and our family "are of God, little children, and have overcome them, because He who is in you is greater than He who is in the world" (I John 4:4).

Also in January of 2006 I learned of a book called *Created to be His Help Meet*[6] by Debi Pearl. Several women in our church were doing the study online with our pastor's daughter. After the third friend invited me to read it, I decided to investigate, thinking this must be from God. I bought the book and began to read. What I learned seemed insightful at first, then it started to step on my toes. I remember closing the book at one point and saying to God that it was too archaic. But the reply came right back. ***"This is truth."*** So, I read on. The book is a detailed account of how to become the godly wife I was created to be, while also including references dealing with abuse and adultery. The author purports that although we as wives have been given the "out" in the case of adultery, we could actually radically trust God to do something new—an incredible healing work from the inside out. She also gives the reader examples of real-life circumstances surrounding divorce and especially divorce involving children.

Unfortunately, this was all too familiar to me. I knew by now what it was like to be divorced, having initially thought that the grass would be greener, only to have discovered it was a putrid shade of brown on the other side. I had always vehemently sworn that if my husband were committing adultery, I would immediately take God's "out" and get a divorce. After reading this, I was not so sure. By the time I finished reading this book, with confidence from God that I was lead to read it and that it was His truth, I determined my path would be a different, more radical one, should this ever be my predicament. I fully believed that God was showing me a different way. I would trust in Him for His healing of my family, should my circumstances ever turn so dire.

The truth was, my situation already *was* dire. At that point in our marriage, we had no intimacy, little communication, and much fighting and violence. We were in a full-blown pattern of codependency and verbal, emotional and other kinds of abuse, though I still didn't fully realize it then. Actually, there were many days, prior to me reading the above-referenced book, that I even prayed for God to show me that my husband was committing adultery, so I could have Biblical grounds to divorce him. But no sign came then. The fighting got worse, though, and was eventually happening frequently in front of our two small children.

In January of 2006, the Lord began warning me that my husband was struggling with lust. We were barely intimate at all at this point, and the violence in our marriage continued. Divorce was a common threat between us. The Lord continued speaking to me about my anger and about my witness to my husband and to our young son, even and especially in the face of danger and hurt and betrayal. He also admonished me about my not letting my husband lead, and about my disrespect for him—showing me that even when I called myself doing the right thing, the "holy" thing, it was unholy if I was not coming under my husband's leadership. God was showing me that I needed to call sin "sin," and that often the very way that I interacted with my husband was disrespectful—arguing and nagging him and pushing for my way—but that I couldn't see my own sin.

The Lord was telling me to pray more and talk less, a lesson that literally took years to sink in. One morning, I heard the Lord say to my heart, ***"Obedience isn't easy; but it is a choice."*** Meanwhile, my husband was filled with bitterness. He blamed everything in our marriage on me. Nothing I could do was good enough to make him love me. He was angry all the time. Thankfully, the Lord was also working on me in the codependency department, teaching me that I couldn't "fix" everything by apologizing for things I was not at fault for—and that I was not always at fault, simply because someone was mad at me. I still needed to walk in truth and with godly boundaries, and to pray without ceasing for my husband and our family. This was a mountain of proportions that only God could move.

By the Lord's love and through His wisdom, we were still in the same incredibly Spirit-filled church with a body of believers who put their faith into action. When they began to see our need, they came out of the woodwork to surround us with prayer and supportive phone calls and godly wisdom and advice learned through their own marital struggles. The women talked with me, and the men called my husband. My own husband, who is an extremely private person, made a remark one day that although normally he hated having anyone in his business, this church had his permission to "mind his business anytime." We were both in awe of the validity of the Gospel as we witnessed this church family in action. We had not known that kind of real love before. God's love was on display here for all to see. What a testimony to His goodness—His Word was being fully lived out before our very eyes. We had been in some counseling up to this point, but eventually we began counseling with some of the pastors of this church. We were blessed to be a part of a body of believers and church leadership who loved God with all of their hearts, souls, minds and strength.

God began preparing me as early as 2006 that the suffering I was enduring was foundational to the work I would do for Him in the future. One day while in my bedroom, I heard the Holy Spirit say to me that I was going through these trials in my marriage to be able to counsel other women. He would later confirm that word to me many times over.

Meanwhile, the Lord was strengthening me and breathing His life into my veins. I read a life-changing book by John and Stasi Eldredge during this time called *Captivating*.[7] In it, Stasi tells us to ask the Lord His name for us. She explains that He has a name for us that only He knows, and encourages us to seek Him to hear what only the Almighty, who fashioned us with His hands, could call His creation. I began seeking Him about this name, His name for me. One morning in February of that same year, as I was praying and just sitting in His presence, He gave it to me. ***"Songbird,"*** He spoke into my spirit. At the exact time I was reading Hosea 2:15, the Holy Spirit illumined my heart. That verse reads "She shall sing there." Actually, the whole context is about a woman scorned by adultery, and how God mercifully draws her back to Himself. Fitting. Hosea 2:14-15 reads, "Therefore, behold, I will allure her, will bring her into the wilderness, and speak comfort to her. I will give her her vineyards from there, and the Valley of Achor as a door of hope; *she shall sing there* (italics mine), as in the days of her youth, as in the day when she came up from the land of Egypt." The Valley of Achor was a very dark place—a place of death and of remembering the Lord's recompense for sin. Wow.

But He didn't stop there. I was listening to a worship song, and the singer sang the word "song" simultaneously as God was telling me my name from His Word. Over the song, I could actually hear birds singing out my window. Then I looked out the window and saw one fly from a treetop nearby. I thanked the Lord for the sweetness and truth that only He could bring. And as a little kiss from my Heavenly Father, right then my cherished son entered the room and hugged me and told me he loved me. I was overflowing. The Lord would confirm the name He gave to me that day over and over again with great certainty in the days and years to come. My journal entry from February 14, 2008 reads, "'Songbirds are taught to sing in the dark.' Oswald Chambers."[8] What a powerful and sweet word from my Heavenly Father.

In March of 2006, God blessed me with another prophetic word over my life. I was facilitating a group of women in a Bible study at our church that year. Our teacher for those several weeks was our pastor's daughter, a gifted speaker and author, but also gifted prophetically. During our prayer time, she began going from person to person, as she felt led by the Holy Spirit, calling out gifts that the Lord was showing her. She stopped before me and called me "prayer warrior." "Silent killer" she called me twice. She said I had no idea of the power inside me. The Lord was certainly moving in a way that only He could understand. But He was moving mountains before my very eyes.

Later, God even blessed me with a vision of our baby girl one night when my husband and I were at a crisis point in our marriage. Things had become so rough, we were not even sleeping in the same room some nights. That particular night, three months pregnant and laying in my bed alone, I was weeping, crying out to God. I remember asking Him to please show me something—anything—to help me hang on, because I could not face all of the despair before me. In that instant, eyes closed but not sleeping, I had a tiny dream of a little baby girl being born. In the days and weeks that followed, I asked God to confirm what I began to realize was a vision from Him. He did in several ways. Our baby girl was born on October 7 of 2006. God truly *had* heard me and answered my prayers from heaven, once again. We were elated to have our beautiful, darling girl, a genuine gift from God that we, once again, did not deserve. Her presence and her radiant joy would bring life to our family in unexpected ways in the years to come.

CHAPTER 6

"For we do not wrestle against flesh and blood, but against principalities, against powers, against the rulers of the darkness of this age, against spiritual hosts of wickedness in the heavenly places. Therefore take up the whole armor of God, that you may be able to withstand in the evil day, and having done all, to stand."

~ Ephesians 6:12-13

By 2007 our financial situation was in complete upheaval. Some days we didn't have enough money to go to the store and buy baby food, milk, or bread. My husband and I were arguing regularly about everything, but money was the main subject. Things were breaking in our home; and we had no money to repair them. In one week, the air conditioning went out, and the shower in the master bath leaked all into our closet. We had to rip up the closet carpet to dry it out. In another week, our cell phones were shut off and the dishwasher was on the fritz. We began asking God if we were supposed to sell our home. We owned three rent houses at the time, but were behind on our mortgage payments for them. We were often robbing Peter to pay Paul. I also was made aware that we were three years behind on our taxes. But God kept providing.

One morning, before it was even light outside, my husband woke me with the news that we were overdrawn. Just the day before, I distinctly heard the Lord tell me, **"Catherine, do not worry about the money. I will provide you with exactly what you need. Your job is to be wise with what I give you."** I remember praying, "Done. Ok, God, I can do that. You just tell us how to spend it and we will. But now I'm confused. We can't spend *nothing* wisely. We can't be good stewards of *nothing*. I began to pray, "God, we need so much right now. We need food. The kids need clothes and shoes. We owe two mortgage payments and *many* bills. I don't even have any makeup (small and inconsequential, yet not to Him!) We need, let's see, $6,000." The number just came into my heart as I was praying. "Ok, God," I said, "I'm not sure if that number came from you or not. I sure don't think I just made it up; but it's possible. If I did and I'm just being vain or proud (which Satan kept telling me I was), I'm sorry. And You certainly don't have to do anything that's not Your will. But if it's from You, then I'd like it—today. Before this weekend. T (my husband) and (our son) are going camping; and they don't even have money for food, or to pay the man in charge (they were going with a church group). I know it sounds impossible; but nothing is impossible with my God. And so I'm asking, if it's Your will."

When I finished praying, I heard the Holy Spirit say, **"Call your husband and ask him to pray too."** I called and left a message on his voice mail at his new job. By 12:30 p.m., my husband called me back to say my prayer was answered. He had received a check for $6,700 from a mortgage deal, and had paid $700 to two people he owed for processing and referral. The remaining amount was $6,000, just as God had prompted me to ask from Him. Just like that. He cares about every detail—big or small—of our lives. We are His beloved. We are His people and the sheep of His pasture. I am still amazed.

In February 2007, I went on a miraculous, heaven-comped trip to Seattle, Washington to stay with my close friend (we will call her "Tracy," later to be known as another of the Soul Sisters) and her family for two weeks to help after the birth of their fourth child. The Lord began showing Tracy and I together one day how to do more spur-of-the-moment ministry. I had been hearing God say, **"Tell them Jesus loves them,"** while she had been hearing the Lord's voice telling her to ask others how she could pray with them. We both gave it a go one day at a shopping mall near her home. It was an exercise in worship and obedience for both of us, no matter what we may have been going through at the time or would go through in the future. God would continue to bless and grow this obedience in us, one situation at a time.

Unveiled

In a continued whirlwind of trials that year God kept showing Himself through and through. In the same week in which we had no money to even buy baby food, God reminded me that now our baby was old enough for me to mash up grown-up food for her to eat. The four of us never went hungry, even when things were at their very worst. One day we had just enough money in the bank to pay the mortgage, but no food in the pantry. My husband and I paid the mortgage and asked God for money for food. By the end of the day, we had received a check in the mail from State Farm, a dividend for $150. Grocery money, compliments of the King of Kings. We even had a dear friend (let's call her "Rhonda") in our church, not coincidentally with a degree in financial counseling, who paid our bills on several occasions over a period of several months. She was truly a God-send. She also took a look at our finances and helped us to begin budgeting God's way. I prayed and prayed through that time for God to teach us good stewardship, that He would fix our wrecked credit, and that we would even have savings for college and retirement someday.

One day I was so incensed at my husband in the height of all this struggle that I dropped a plastic-potted plant over the balcony onto him as he lay watching TV on the couch. In my (distorted!) mind, I thought I just couldn't take it anymore. I'd become disgruntled, despairing of our relationship, and hopeless about our future together. Expecting him to come pounding through the game room door after that little escapade, I waited—angry and shaking. When I came downstairs a little while later to apologize, I saw the plant just sitting on the floor beside him, like he'd just calmly set it aside and kept watching TV. I remorsefully apologized and asked forgiveness of him, then of God. And I felt a twinge of anxiety, like maybe now it would take us that much longer to get to this other place God was trying to take us, because I had backslidden so much. But then God said *"No."* Jesus said, ***"Receive My peace. You are forgiven."*** And I did. And I was. And I am.

God was showing us that these trials were about so much more than money and learning how to use it. For me, they were about learning how to come under my husband's leadership, and to trust God to lead him, even if I couldn't see that happening right in front of me. And God kept pouring His truth into me, day after day. The story of Jonah, Psalm 34, Isaiah 64:4, Proverbs 21:1, Isaiah 57:17-19, Psalm 46, Zephaniah 3:14-17 were just a few of the passages the Lord gave me over and over. I knew a lot of this struggle was about the Lord turning my husband's heart, but I didn't know the full extent of what He was turning it from. God kept showing and speaking the word ***"foundation"*** to me; I soon came to understand that He wanted to rebuild the very foundation we were standing on. It was a daily walk, really a minute-by-minute dependency on Him. I started anointing our entire home with oil that year and praying scripture over our home and family. I began to understand that no one else loved me more. No one else loved my kids or my husband more.

And I began to absolutely adore my Abba, my King. I loved Him more every day, and I was hungering and thirsting for His Word. God would not let us go, no matter how immature and flawed we were, because of His great love for us.

As I bathed our children one night, I saw a picture of God loving me like I love my children—but so much more. Actually, the first picture I had is of how much He loved them and was taking care of them, and that He would not let them go. Then I began to realize that our Father loved my husband and me in that same way, the same unconditional way that we love our children—but greater and more perfectly. He had not forgotten us or the details, however messy and scary they were, of the trials we were going through. He knew exactly what we were going through and just how painful it was for us, and it was painful for Him too. He hurts when His children hurt. And He would revive us again, for His Name's sake and for His glory.

On November 1, 2007, I had a dream. God was telling me in the dream that I was about to be in a horrific car accident; but I must go through it for His glory. I woke up terrified.

have a dining room here, and many more happy memories in this home I've given you." The very next day our pre-school son's enrollment fee for the following year at his Christian school was paid by my husband's best friend. God was continuing to provide for our family, despite our current bleak financial circumstances.

On Valentine's day in February 2008, as I was walking through the grocery store while fasting for breakthrough for our family, I heard the Lord telling me to tell the woman in the shopping aisle that Jesus loved her. Just that morning I had told the Lord how grateful I was, overjoyed even, that He would orchestrate the details of our lives to have my mother-in-law call and offer to buy our son's valentines and candy to hand out to his classmates. We were that broke. And here I was in Walmart, resenting all of the penny pinching, and God was telling me to love on a stranger for Him—and I was struggling. Tired and stressed about our money and our current situation, I began to think of Paul, who never needed a reason to praise our God. So in a moment, I told the lady we passed in the aisle that Jesus loved her. She said, "Thank you." Then a moment later, she turned around again and said, "Thank you for saying that." I said something small and insignificant back, still in my selfish struggle in my head. I started thinking, "I really need someone to say it to *me*." Then out of the blue, my sweet baby girl riding shotgun in the grocery cart began grabbing my face in her passionate, fun-loving way. She was hugging me and kissing me with all her might. And she wouldn't let go. I couldn't help but laugh and tell her, and my Jesus, "I love you too." Then I started to cry. She was still holding on, hugging me and loving me. I'll never forget it.

God was teaching us how to trust Him and to *praise Him* above all else, even when there are no cattle lowing in the stalls (Habakkuk 3:17-19). Then on the morning of February 20, I clearly heard God whisper in my ear as I was bent over cleaning out the cats' litter box as part of my early morning routine. I heard very plainly the word, ***"Zerubbabel."*** I had no idea what that meant, but knew it had a Biblical reference. When I looked the word up in my index, I discovered its origin in the book of Haggai, in the place I was already reading. God called Zerubbabel His signet ring. He was the son of Shealtiel, and governor of Judah. He was also the rebuilder of the Jewish temple, 48 years after its destruction by Nebuchadnezzar and the Babylonians (Haggai 2:23, Ezra 5:2,11).

Little did I know God was calling me to be His Zerubbabel.

As things progressed and seemed to get more and more difficult, I regularly bowed my head to my Lord and King, begging Him for mercy and to speak to me in a way that I could understand and know that He understood my heart. One such day, as I was struggling to be understood by my earthly husband, God played a song on the XM-TV radio station just for me called, "Flesh of My Flesh."[9] At that moment, I heard my Heavenly Father say, **"I've given you this man as your husband because I love you."** And then, **"I am your Husband. You are the bride of Christ. You are flesh of My flesh, bone of My bone. We are one."**

On February 22, 2008, I was awakened by a loud knocking, three times, at 4:30 in the morning. Startled, I got out of bed to find my husband already on the couch, watching TV. He was also startled by the rap at the door. He asked me if I wanted him to go outside; I said no. We looked through the windows, and he checked the garage door, and found nothing. Either God was trying to get our attention—or someone else was. I prayed for God's protection over our family and to be in His will.

The more the gap widened between my husband and me, the more I realized I too was struggling with lust. I often found myself focusing on a random man who seemed to be the godly head of his home, wondering what it would be like to be married to such a one. I was constantly taking this to the Lord in prayer, and rebuking the enemy, the spirit of lust specifically, out loud in Jesus' name. I often had strange dreams of other men, not necessarily sexual. The overriding premise was that I was loved and adored and cared for, far above all other women. When I awoke from these dreams, I immediately felt depressed and hopeless, often longing to go back to my dream world where I knew I would be cherished. Once I got up and began to start my day, those depressed feelings often turned to shame. I battled the enemy just about every morning in prayer to God as I started each day, having been attacked in some way, the night or wee hours of the morning before in my thoughts and dreams.

God was also showing me that I struggled with making people bigger than Him. Because we went to a mega-church, where sometimes some of the people—congregational and leadership—seemed larger than life, I found myself getting nervous or insecure around various ones for a multitude of reasons. Interestingly enough, this was contradictory to a principle I upheld in our family—I taught our son, and would later teach our daughter, not to put people before God or to change their behavior in any way based on what the crowd thought or what peers were doing. Yet I was clearly struggling with this insecurity myself. Easier said than done, I guess. I repented to the Lord then, but realized it would probably be an ongoing process as He broke me of these sinful thoughts and wrong motives.

Simultaneously, God was telling me to be sober and vigilant. He gave me 1 Peter 1:13 over and over. I began to understand that God wanted me to be fully aware, completely alert to His teaching and to the Holy Spirit's prompting at all times, but especially now.

Oddly enough, during this time, my husband seemed to be inundated with opportunities to join Bible studies in various forms—old friends who resurfaced and invited him to join their groups, men leading Bible studies at his new job, and the men's fellowship breakfast at our church. He participated somewhat, continuing to keep me abreast of the ways God kept "showing up."

On February 28th of that year, the Lord gave me a vision of how they saw me in heaven. The angels knew me well as one of the worshippers. God called me "**special, His girl, set apart.**" They rejoiced and sang around me and around my family. They protected our family. Whoa.

Through all of this struggle and pain, God was showing me some pretty big blessings all along the way. One day when we finally got paid, I was out running errands like a crazy woman with our five-year-old son in tow. I was truly grateful to finally have had a little money to breathe, and I was even able to get glasses and contacts because of the recent incoming funds. But as I pulled into the driveway, completely worn out from all of this running around, a thought popped into my head. One of the greatest blessings of *not* having the money was the peace and quiet at home with our family. My husband and daughter were just relaxing at home all of that day (it was a Saturday), having a wonderful time together. I on the other hand, was grumpy with the children late in the day because of all of the tasks I had laid on myself that afternoon. I repented to the Lord, asking His forgiveness once again for not resting in His peace. It is always there for the asking. We just need to receive it.

By this time, our five-year-old son was old enough, and smart enough, to perceive some of what was going on and to ask us intelligent, thought-provoking questions. In response to his query regarding God's character one day, I replied that the Lord gives us everything, and He even gave Daddy to me and allowed us to fall in love and then allowed us to get married. I explained that He gave us to each other and then He gave us our beautiful family. To which my son quickly retorted, "Are you still in love?" My answer was yes, that I would always be in love with his daddy. He looked puzzled, and I asked him if he thought we weren't in love. He then asked, "Even though you fight?" I told him that we would always be in love. Ouch. Out of the mouths of babes.

On March 11, 2008, the Lord told me two times in the morning not to be disobedient to the heavenly vision (Acts 26:19). He showed me the passage in Acts 16 about Paul being given a vision in the night by God to go to Macedonia, and this after the Holy Spirit closed a door in Asia and again in Bithynia, not permitting Paul and his men to continue their journey there. When Paul and crew sailed several days' journey to Macedonia, they were immediately engaged in several God-appointed activities. These appointments ultimately landed them in jail, from whence the famous chain-breaking, jail-shaking exit occurred. Had Paul not obeyed the Lord initially in changing the entire course of his journey, that jailer and his family would never have believed on the name of the Lord Jesus Christ for salvation from their sins; and an entire army would have missed the witness of the Holy Spirit and the miracle of the gospel (Acts 16:6-40). I knew the Lord was telling me He would show me what to do; and I was absolutely to obey, beyond all cost-counting or logical fears. I had to obey God's voice no matter what. Concurrently, the Lord was also waking me up a lot to pray in the middle of the night, around 3 and 4 a.m.

One night after a particularly awful fight with my husband, I was upstairs pouting and then decided to sleep there. Frustrated beyond words, I kept pouring my heart out to the Lord in anguish and despair. I clearly heard the Lord say at that moment, ***"Do not give up. You're closer than you think. Do not give up now."*** In fact, it was then that I turned on the TV in the game room, needing to cool my jets, and *Facing the Giants*[10] was on again. God had been telling me that He was my giant-slayer, giving me this movie for reference more than once, along with a Beth Moore Bible study on the life of David, and another study I found at home by Max

Lucado called *Facing Your Giants*.[11] At every turn, my Lord and Savior was reminding me that He was bigger than all that was before me, bigger and stronger than every evil giant in my life.

March 20, 2008, a woman left a message on our home answering machine, accusing my husband of calling her. This was not the first strange message we had received from this woman. I began a fast. The Lord showed me, along with many other strengthening scriptures**,** Micah 7:7-10, "Therefore I will look to the LORD; I will wait for the God of my salvation; my God will hear me. Do not rejoice over me, my enemy; when I fall, I will arise. When I sit in darkness, the LORD will be a light to me. I will bear the indignation of the LORD, because I have sinned against Him, until He pleads my case and executes justice for me, He will bring me forth to the light; I will see His righteousness. Then *she who is* my enemy will see, and shame will cover her who said to me, 'Where is the LORD your God?' My eyes will see her; Now she will be trampled down like mud in the streets."

On March 24th, 2008 around 5 a.m., I awoke to let our dog out. I thought about getting up to have time with the Lord, but decided to go back to bed because I was too sleepy. Right then, I heard a frightening noise, I can only describe it by saying Satan swooshed in. It sounded like demons roaring in the distance. I told myself I imagined it, and went back to sleep. By mid-morning I knew it was not my imagination. I had a horrifying dream to start my day, and then was completely spiritually attacked the entire day, constantly praying and trusting the Lord to rescue me, which He did. I kept thinking, too, about this stalker person and the strange events that had been taking place at our home and whether or not my husband was actually having an affair. I kept praying and asking the Lord's protection. I knew I could trust Him to take care of my family, even in the most alarming and terrifying of circumstances. Clearly, I was going to need to be on my guard and on my knees from now on. The enemy was prowling about like a roaring lion, seeking whom he might devour (1 Peter 5:8). I trusted my Lord to protect my family and me.

As the spiritual and physical/emotional struggle continued, the horrific dreams continued. One morning the Lord woke me at 3:38 from a nightmare. I was so grateful to be free from the attacker who plagued me in my dreams. I got out of bed immediately and went into my guest bedroom where I frequently spent time alone with God. God gave me Revelation 4-5 that morning. As I read and prayed, I realized that this is exactly how *He* saw me, which is just what I prayed He would show me when I got into my chair. Revelation 5:9-10 says, "You are worthy to take the scroll, and to open its seals; for You were slain, and have redeemed us to God by Your blood out of every tribe and tongue and people and nation, and have made us kings and priests to our God; and we shall reign on the earth." I fell down on my face in worship. The tears would not stop flowing. I just kept thinking, "So this is what my mom saw the *instant* she left this earth. This is what she's seeing right now." I imagined her saying to herself, "How in the world did I believe those lies Satan told me all of those years about myself?! This is my home!!!" And I realized my GG and Gramps and Mamaw were all seeing Him too, and worshipping Him in all honor and power and glory. Wow. I just kept praising Him and saying, "I'm not worthy." I knew that day—He loved me *so* much. By His wounds, I was healed.

Another morning soon after, the Lord woke me at 2:47 a.m. I came into my quiet time room and lay prostrate on the floor and blessed His name. I praised Him and loved Him and thanked Him. He gave me Psalm 138-139. He had me read the verses aloud. I especially focused on verses 15-16 of chapter 139 which say, "My frame was not hidden from You when I was made in secret, and skillfully wrought in the lowest parts of the earth. Your eyes saw my substance being yet unformed. And in Your book they were all written, the days fashioned for me, when *as yet there were* none of them." Later that morning at church, our beloved pastor read the same verse. Tears rolled down my cheeks and my heart leaped. I told the Lord, "I love You, my Father, my Adonai."

CHAPTER 8

"Come, and let us return to the LORD; for He has torn, but He will heal us; He has stricken, but He will bind us up. After two days He will revive us; on the third day He will raise us up, that we may live in His sight. Let us know, let us pursue the knowledge of the LORD. His going forth is established as the morning; He will come to us like the rain, like the latter and *former rain to the earth."*

~ Hosea 6:1-3

On March 21st, the Lord woke me in the wee hours to pray. I did so, obediently, falling asleep over and over in my chair with my Bible. The Lord woke me up with the words, ***"three weeks from Wednesday."*** According to my calendar, that would fall on April 16.

On April 10, 2008, we had a terrible storm. Our power went out, and our favorite big shade tree cracked in half in our backyard. Under this very tree, the children and I had enjoyed many a picnic lunch and spent countless hours rolling on the grass, laughing and giggling and telling stories. I was crying and upset with the Lord when it hit me. That tree had fallen sideways, hurting nothing and no one. It could have easily been one of the large trees closer to our house *falling on our house* on our bedroom, injuring (or killing) both my husband and me, and possibly our children. "Even the winds and the sea obey Him" (Matthew 8:27). God was not short on ways to get our attention.

My grandfather died April 11 of 2008. On the day he died, in the afternoon preceding his death, I received a letter in the mail from the

Christian school our son attended. By this point, we had applied for financial aid, but were told that we needed to get some more financial documents in order to be able to be considered for aid. I was expecting that this letter from the school was more of the same, an explanation of why we were not being awarded aid at this time. To my complete surprise, when I tore open the letter, it read that his school was awarding us the *full 50% maximum financial aid benefit.* Period. Done. I fell on my face sobbing, and the words "thank you" could not even come out right away, because of my sobbing. The floor was wet. I served an awesome God, and He was taking care of my family.

Grandpa's funeral was eye-opening for my husband and me. The week before we were to be married, my husband had received a call from my grandfather, urging him not to marry me. My husband is a black man and I am a white woman, and you can imagine this did not sit well with us. My grandfather had explained at the time that it was not about us, but about our children, and that he was concerned they would have trouble growing up. Needless to say, we had not listened that day and had been all too upset by the situation over the years that followed. I had forgiven Grandpa, but had also had a lot of trouble relating to him after that. My husband had just chosen not to deal with him unless it was absolutely necessary.

Well, lo and behold, at Grandpa's funeral, the pallbearers were six black men from the Union Gospel Mission where he had served faithfully every week for the better part of his life, after he had returned home from the war. My husband and I were stunned. We left the funeral in shock and deep sorrow.

That night found us huddled on the couch, discussing Grandpa and his life and what all of this meant. Something was said that reminded me of a funny story about Grandpa, and I told my husband. He remembered, and we laughed together. We remarked about how wonderful the service was and how perfectly and joyfully his life was celebrated. My husband was particularly impressed with the superintendent of the Union Gospel Mission who had given a lengthy, eloquent and edifying speech, full of loving, fond and kind words about Grandpa. This man was also a black man. My great uncle had also spoken, followed by the pastor of the Spanish church founded by Granny and Grandpa. The service couldn't have been more moving. My husband was confused. "Surely, if all these men of color loved him," he said,

"I had to have missed something." I told him I kept having the same thought over and over at the funeral. He said he wanted to hear what it was and not to hold back. I told him I kept hearing in my head, "It's for the kids." We both agreed that the words, "It's about your children" meant just that.

Grandpa had come from a day and age when people didn't mix races in marriage, and he had seen lots of awfulness over the years concerning race relations. He had truly not wanted that for us, or for our children. That fateful phone call had been seven years before. Seven years of misunderstanding ensued. Grandpa had to die for our eyes be open to the truth. It hurt a lot.

I was so grateful that Grandpa was with the Lord. He was verily a man of great faith and loved the Lord deeply. He just had trouble conveying his thoughts in a loving manner sometimes. He was tactfully challenged. But he still loved me, us, and wanted the best for us. It was really healing to have had this conversation with my husband, albeit a little too late. I was painfully aware that my husband did understand once and for all who my grandfather truly was, and that he knew there was no harm meant. I sobbed knowing that we could not get him back. There was no time left this side of heaven to be able to tell Grandpa I loved him, and that I finally understood. I do believe that the Lord used his passing to open our eyes, and to bring some healing and understanding to our lives and to our marriage. The next day, I journaled this eye-opening experience. It was *April 16, Wednesday.*

On April 20, 2008, my husband awoke at 3 a.m. from a dream in which the words, **"I will repay the years the locusts have eaten"** were being repeated over and over. When we finally rose for the day, a slight panic began to set in. We had to empty the kids' piggybanks for milk, bread, and cat food money. My husband then suggested I withdraw a sizeable sum of money from our son's savings at the bank. I did so, crying all the way to the bank. We argued a little in the morning, both feeling the pressure. I continued to ask God for a miracle. Around noon, my husband got the mail. There were about twenty envelopes—a six-months old back-load of mail, originally sent to the wrong address. Included was a check for $1,050 from one of our old tenants. Once again, I stood amazed at my Jehovah Jireh.

On May 17, 2008, I had a dream. I was in the top story of a 100-story building. I owed rent for my space there; but I couldn't pay. The people who owned the building were going to implode it with me inside, if I did not pay them what I owed them by a certain date. As the date quickly approached, I knew God would save me, but I didn't know how. I kept telling everyone this—but they all just ignored me, thinking I was about to die. The day finally came, and they did blow up the building with me in it. But I did not die. I escaped with my life. Somehow the base was still standing and I was able to get out of the structure in time. But in the days that followed, I noticed a strange phenomenon. Not one of my closest family members or friends noticed the miraculous escape God had granted me. Even people passing by the half blown-up building just ignored it and walked on by. It was up to me to tell people how great God was and what He had saved me from—how I should have been dead, but for His grace. Even as I began to tell my story, many listeners seemed apathetic. I was amazed and saddened by their response. Then one day that followed all of this mysterious miracle and it's telling, a funny thing happened. I had the opportunity to go back up to the top of that crazy, blown-up building (the middle was wreckage, but if you went in carefully you could still reach the top) to partake in something not so holy with some members of my extended family. Because I wanted them to love me and accept me, I participated. We made it out alive, without the building falling on us, but I knew I had been stupid and careless. And I knew I had dishonored my Lord. I had gone back to the very site He had raised me from, saved me from, looked Him in the face and said, "It doesn't matter." I felt remorseful. Awful. I knew I was wrong and that I could not dishonor Him that way again. Next time I might not be so blessed as to escape with my life.

You see, He didn't have to save me. He didn't have to raise me from the pit I was in. He didn't have to mercifully step in and lovingly spare my life. But He did. And others needed to know it. And it was up to me to tell them, not to get caught up in worldliness, worrying about what others thought and going along with them. I loved the Lord and it should show. "Everybody oughta know who Jesus is" as our young son often sang. Yes, everybody oughta know who my Jesus is.

Little did I know what my God was preparing me for.

As time went on, the danger signs in my marriage became more frequent. But now even I couldn't see what I was looking for. I found mystery restaurant receipts and was alerted to a separate electric bill with a different address under my husband's name. One day I even drove to the address looking for some shred of anything to convict my husband. I found a small house with a child's bicycle in the front yard. I just drove away shaking and realizing I didn't even know what I was looking for. When I asked my husband questions, I was met with anger and defense and non-definitive answers. At one point, I even made a list with "evidence" on one side, which was severely stacking up; but on the other side I just wrote, "JESUS." Then the phone calls started. The crazy messages from the woman had been continuing. But on this day, someone began prank calling me repeatedly and hanging up. One day for hours on end my cell phone and home phone were constantly ringing together until I just unplugged and turned off all phones.

At one point, a detective helped me obtain what we thought was the address from the phone number I had on caller id. I asked my husband to go with me, and we drove to the house and scared some poor woman to death with the story when she opened the door. It was clearly the wrong house, and I felt like I was beginning to lose my mind. Another day, someone left a note threatening my family under our front door mat. The police were called again and a report was filed. Our family was in disarray and my marriage was in an uproar. I was frantic, and my husband was trying to calm me down, but to no avail. God was beginning to open my eyes to the truth, but I wasn't ready to accept it. He kept taking me to the book of Hosea, and even telling me not to throw my pearls before swine (Matthew 7:6). He was lovingly holding me in His arms of protection (Isaiah 54:10-15).

On July 21, I had a dream in which I heard the words, **"Genesis 28:12."** This is the story of Jacob's ladder in *his* dream, reaching to heaven, with angels ascending and descending on it. In this dream, God stands above the ladder and tells Jacob, "I *am* the LORD God of Abraham your father and the God of Isaac; the land on which you lie I will give to you and your descendants. Also your descendants shall be as the dust of the earth; you shall spread abroad to the west and the east, to the north and the south; and in you and in your seed all the families of the earth shall be blessed. Behold, I *am* with you and will keep you wherever you go, and will bring you back to this land; for I will not leave you until I have done what I have spoken to you" (Genesis 28:12-22).

As God was preparing me for what was about to happen in my marriage, He was giving me His promise of His everlasting care and provision for my family, no matter what. Not ironically, this very year turned out to be a chaotic turning point for most of our country. That same weekend, I was in Waco with my aunt and uncle, for some much-needed r & r, with the kids. My uncle told me that Kay Arthur had prophesied that the Lord would send famine to our land. I began praying and asking God if this were indeed true. He took me to a place in 2 Kings chapter 8, verse 1 where it is written, "…for the LORD has called for a famine, and furthermore, it will come upon the land for seven years." I continued during that time period to seek confirmation from the Lord about that famine; and He continued to give it. I began praying that the Lord would break up our fallow ground, that our hearts would break with what breaks His heart, and that I would mourn over my sin and the sins of our nation. That year was the mortgage and housing crisis of 2008. This financial crisis would last until the end of 2015, seven years later.

My husband was in the mortgage business by that time; and everyone in the housing industry was losing their shirts. He began asking me to look for work. On July 26, our bankruptcy was finalized. Our bank accounts had been frozen for a week so the change could take place. We often had little or no money in the bank. At one point, we had $25 for a week. Our son needed shoes, and we had re-enrolled him in his Christian school without knowing where the money for his tuition would come from. Miraculously, in the same day that I told my husband our son needed shoes, our son was given some gently-worn shoes by a friend. Then our neighbor, who worked for Steak & Ale and had recently lost his job, brought over 42 pounds of Black Angus steak. Over and over again, we saw God work miracle after miracle, as I fasted and prayed and waited on Him. I began temporarily working some wholesale markets. That summer should have been one of the most stress-producing seasons. But in fact, it was the exact opposite. I began to understand that God's "manna" was actually all we ever needed for life and joy. I stayed in His Word constantly. To feel His peace was truly miraculous in the face of such a grave storm.

The following entry from my journal dated September 26, 2008 provides a good explanation for what was going on in our lives at that time:

"I can't believe I've forgotten to write this until now. Last week, God truly showed up & showed <u>out</u> in my family. At the beginning of the week, Sep. 15, T was paid $1,000. But that was all & we had <u>so</u> much to pay. We owed $767 to the electric co. & then almost $1,000 in other bills by the end of the week. He wanted to put it all on his dad's credit card again, but we did that last month. I didn't want to keep living off credit. I asked him if we could just pay the electric bill & then trust God to provide the rest. Reluctantly, he said ok. Well, the 11th hour was approaching, and I didn't have my answer. I began getting antsy. I told the Lord I felt let down even though the deadline was not there yet. Because of my own anxieties and the fact that I had no answer on Wednesday or Thursday, I panicked. But HE obviously was still in control. We had a budget meeting with Rhonda on Wednesday, and she suggested we apply for benevolence with the church. Not at all what either of us had expected. On Thursday, she and I were discussing the church option and the deadlines we faced and my prayers of panic to the Lord. Rhonda, her husband out of work for a year now, gave us the money to pay our overdue bills, including (our son's) school *plus* $100 for savings. HE is <u>so</u> awesome. I wept and wept on the phone with Rhonda. What a dear friend. I pray the LORD will richly bless her and her marriage and her family. Yesterday, my friend J gave me a thank-you card for praying for her marriage & for being a friend. In it was $100, designated specifically so T & I could go on a date! Again, I was on my face before the Lord. <u>What</u> an awesome God. It even came on the day before my garage sale, when I needed change for the buyers! I am praying we can go on this date tonight.

Rhonda gave us over $900 and J gave us $100. He is <u>so</u> faithful. His storehouses are <u>never</u> empty. I love You, Lord!!!"

Followed by this journal entry on September 28th:

"The Lord is definitely sending <u>famine</u> to our land. It has already begun. The financial markets are in the toilet. AIG has collapsed & is requiring a bailout that now the whole country will pay for, to the tune of $10,000 in taxes per family. Lehman Brothers has gone under. Everywhere you look there is unemployment & people are being laid off, (my sister) and (my sister-in-law) included. T can barely make a dime. It is our nation's judgment because of our great sin & rebellion against God. God continues to tell me to bless my family & pray blessings over them & put His name on them. I do. I will continue to. Our family, my children, will be safe. He *will* deliver us. He will reward us according to the cleanness of our hands. Because we are blameless in His sight. God, I am begging You to save my husband."

In September of 2008 God began speaking to me about wheat. By October, I understood Him to say I was to plant the wheat. He confirmed the word about wheat over and over again for the next couple of weeks. This concept seemed so foreign to me, as I was definitely NOT a farmer in any sense of the word. I didn't have a green thumb, or even a turquoise one.

But I would obey. If I had learned anything from God at this point, it was obedience. That was a non-negotiable between the Lord and me. He often told me to do strange things, yet I was always blessed by doing them if I would simply obey. I learned to trust Him because He was (and is!) my Maker and He knew the way that I took better than I.

So, I began researching this garden of wheat. I went to the local feed store in the town where we lived and began to inquire. I learned that it definitely was wheat planting season, right then, at that very time of the year. And that was interesting, because to my knowledge most crops were planted in the spring. The store was out of wheat but offered me a similar product. No, I would wait for them to order the wheat since that is what God told me to plant. I continued to pray during that time that the Lord would speak to me about the wheat. When the man from the feed company called to tell me the wheat was in, I prayed again that the Lord would confirm that I was to plant it before I went to pick it up.

The next morning, the Lord led me to Exodus 9:32 where it is written, "…but the wheat and spelt were not struck (with the Egyptian plagues and pestilence) for they are late crops." Interestingly, God had also continued to give me the story of Moses, Pharaoh and the exodus from Egypt during that time. I understood this to be His confirmation to me. I bought the wheat, and we began planting. I had continued to pray about the size and location of the garden of wheat God wanted me to plant. My husband (reluctantly—yes, it was a little weird) dug a 4 x 4 plot for us to plant the wheat, and the children and I planted the seeds a few days later. We didn't understand then what it was for. We just planted our garden as an altar to Him. We wanted to honor Him with what we had.

The verse the Lord gave me several times then was John 12:24, "Most assuredly, I say to you, unless a grain of wheat falls into the ground and dies, it remains alone; but if it dies, it produces much grain." He also showed me that the wheat was to feed the hungry. He showed me in Isaiah 58:7 and Ezekiel 18:7 that I was to bring to my house the poor who are cast out, and to cover the naked with clothing. I would come to understand over the next several years how God truly intended for my family to implement this.

Journal entry October 16, 2008:

"The Lord is absolutely, positively giving us our daily bread. Yesterday my 'check engine oil' light came on—not the light that's supposed to tell me to *change* my oil, but the one that comes on when you've missed that. We just got paid, but the money is already appropriated for other things. (Our daughter) was sick yesterday & I asked S (friend) to bring (our son) home from school. I also told her about the oil light. She asked me if I had the money to change my oil. To which I started to reply 'yes' & then had to honestly say 'no.' She gave me a check for $50 which will cover my oil change and the $27 overdraft fee we got yesterday because T and I both got $50 of gas when we should have waited one more day. The day before, (our son's) friend and his mom came to play with us, at 5:30 pm., & brought us 2 pizzas for dinner. A few days before that S gave me some pumpkin bread. The day or so before that, A (dear, next-door neighbor friend) brought us a tray of sandwiches from McAllister's left over from a meeting at her church. A couple of days before that, S paid me $10 for the $5 book I'd bought for her. She also gave us a bunch of (her daughter's) clothes for (our daughter). Rhonda sent, and is sending, lots of (her daughter's) clothes for (our daughter). T's mom sent us home with spaghetti that fed us for several days. (My father-in-law) bought (our daughter's) birthday cake—I prayed and he offered. My dad bought $62 worth of steak and potato and party 'fixin's', and we had enough steaks to feed 12 people because of what (our next-door neighbors) brought over a couple of months ago. We had <u>just</u> enough potatoes, lettuce, tomatoes, dressing and croutons for a wonderful salad. We had an <u>elaborate</u> meal for (our daughter's) birthday, with *no* money. J and W (friends) bought us dinner and a movie—what a treat that was. C (sweet next-door neighbor on the other side) brought over some okra from her garden this past weekend which completed our fried fish meal. I forgot to mention the $10 S gave us paid for (our daughter's) diapers and (our son's) poster board for his school project and snacks for his class that week. And on and on and on. I woke up this morning with this song playing over and over in my dream,

> *'Holy, holy, holy*
> *is the LORD God almighty*

> *who was and is*
> *and is to come.'*

Revelation 4:8
2 Chronicles 20:15,17"

Also, a few days later, the church approved Rhonda's recommendation to give us $2,478 to keep our car from being repossessed. Our financial counselor friend told us that they almost never approved benevolence spending for cars. Clearly, God gave them a different answer in our case. Just days after that, my sister told us she was giving us $1,400 as her tithe money for the following month. We were literally standing still and seeing "the salvation of the LORD" which HE was accomplishing for us today (Exodus 14:13-14).

I am literally still in awe and weeping as I am writing this book and recounting this time. To say "God is good" is a gross understatement. I can't begin to fathom the words I would truly use to describe Him.

CHAPTER 9

""For I," says the LORD, "will be a wall of fire all around her, and I will be the glory in her midst.""

~ Zechariah 2:5

Since 2006, God had been giving me the same passage of scripture in Isaiah 57, verses 18-19, which says, "'I have seen his ways, and will heal him; I will also lead him, and restore comforts to him and to his mourners. I create the fruit of the lips: Peace, peace to *him who is* far off and to *him who is* near,' says the LORD, 'and I will heal him.'" I didn't exactly know what to do with these words, or what it all meant. But I knew my marriage was in trouble, and that my husband was getting further and further away from me. And further away from God. God was apparently already dealing with him too, unbeknown to me. He had lost two jobs in one year and our finances were completely drained.

Then on November 7, 2008, an answer came. I was in a prayer group with three other women. We had been meeting weekly for several weeks to pray over our children and over their school. That day after our meeting, we took a slight diversion and began talking about our marriages. One of them posed the question, "So what would you do if you discovered your husband was cheating on you?" One by one, we all gave our different answers, most of them sounding similar and ending with the eventual "leaving" outcome. I went last. My answer was different on that day than I ever thought it would be, I explained. I told of the book by Debi Pearl the Lord had shown me to read in 2006, and of the radical viewpoints detailed there. I explained how God had changed my thought patterns to this understanding, this belief, that He could actually heal even this most traumatic wound in marriage. They listened, and one by one gave their varying opinions of my newfound radicalism. One woman could kind of see my viewpoint, but wasn't sure she'd have the guts to carry it out. Another just thought I was bonkers. One friend didn't think I was quite so crazy.

I drove home from our meeting that day with one burning question for God: "Is this, indeed, happening to me??" My heart was beating out of my chest, and my stomach was churning as the inquiry left my lips.

As I parked my car in the garage and opened our back door, the phone was ringing. I saw the caller i.d.—it was the counselor at our church that my husband and I had been seeing for several months. We had not seen him in several weeks by that point. This counselor had previously confronted my husband about adultery in his office, but my husband had denied the accusation. I answered the phone and told our counselor what I thought was happening. He agreed. I told him I was going to get in the Word and talk to God to get some answers. He agreed.

I immediately went upstairs to our guest bedroom where I spent lots of time in prayer and in God's Word. I asked God to show me, please, and in no uncertain terms, what was happening in my marriage—if my husband was indeed committing adultery. I opened my Bible directly to Psalm 50. I was shaking as I read my Bible, terrified of what I might hear God saying to me that day. When I skimmed the chapter and found no immediate answer to my question, I felt the Holy Spirit say, ***"Go back."*** Regretfully, I did, and my eyes landed on verse 18, which talks about consenting with thieves and partaking with adulterers. I knew I had my answer. My heart felt like it would come right out of my chest. But then, the Lord directed me to another passage in the Psalms. I turned right to Psalm 18. God's loving reply to me is written below.

> "I will love You, O LORD, my strength.
> The LORD is my rock and my fortress and my deliverer;
> My God, my strength, in whom I will trust;
> My shield and the horn of my salvation, my stronghold.
> I will call upon the LORD, *who is worthy* to be praised;
> So shall I be saved from my enemies.
> The pangs of death surrounded me,

And the floods of ungodliness made me afraid.
The sorrows of Sheol surrounded me;
The snares of death confronted me.
In my distress I called upon the LORD,
And cried out to my God;
He heard my voice from His temple,
And my cry came before Him, even to His ears.
Then the earth shook and trembled;
The foundations of the hills also quaked and were shaken,
Because He was angry.
Smoke went up from His nostrils,
And devouring fire from His mouth;
Coals were kindled by it.
He bowed the heavens also and came down
With darkness under His feet.
And He rode upon a cherub and flew;
He flew upon the wings of the wind.
He made darkness His secret place;
His canopy around Him *was* dark waters
And thick clouds of the skies.
From the brightness before Him,
His thick clouds passed with hailstones and coals of fire.
The LORD thundered from heaven,
And the Most High uttered His voice,
Hailstones and coals of fire.
He sent out His arrows and scattered the foe,
Lightnings in abundance, and He vanquished them.
Then the channels of the sea were seen,
The foundations of the world were uncovered
At Your rebuke, O LORD,
At the blast of the breath of Your nostrils.
He sent from above, He took me;
He drew me out of many waters.
He delivered me from my strong enemy,
From those who hated me,
For they were too strong for me.

They confronted me in the day of my calamity,
But the LORD was my support.
He also brought me out into a broad place;
He delivered me because He delighted in me.
The LORD rewarded me according to my righteousness;
According to the cleanness of my hands
He has recompensed me.
For I have kept the ways of the LORD,
And have not wickedly departed from my God.
For all His judgments were before me,
And I did not put away His statutes from me.
I was also blameless before Him,
And I kept myself from my iniquity.
Therefore the LORD has recompensed me according to my righteousness;
According to the cleanness of my hands in His sight.
With the merciful You will show Yourself merciful;
With a blameless man You will show Yourself blameless;
With the pure You will show Yourself pure;
And with the devious You will show Yourself shrewd.
For You will save the humble people,
But will bring down haughty looks.
For You will light my lamp;
The LORD my God will enlighten my darkness.
For by You I can run against a troop,
By my God I can leap over a wall.
As for God, His way is perfect;
The word of the LORD is proven;
He is a shield to all who trust in Him.
For who is God, except the LORD?
And who is a rock, except our God?
It is God who arms me with strength,
And makes my way perfect.
He makes my feet like the *feet of* deer,
And sets me on my high places.
He teaches my hands to make war,

So that my arms can bend a bow of bronze.
You have also given me the shield of Your salvation;
Your right hand has held me up,
Your gentleness has made me great.
You enlarged my path under me,
So my feet did not slip.
I have pursued my enemies and overtaken them;
Neither did I turn back again till they were destroyed.
I have wounded them,
So that they could not rise;
They have fallen under my feet.
For You have armed me with strength for the battle;
You have subdued under me those who rose up against me.
You have also given me the necks of my enemies,
So that I destroyed those who hated me.
They cried out, but *there was* none to save;
Even to the LORD, but He did not answer them.
Then I beat them as fine as the dust before the wind;
I cast them out like dirt in the streets.
You have delivered me from the strivings of the people;
You have made me the head of the nations;
A people I have not known shall serve me.
As soon as they hear of me they obey me;
The foreigners submit to me.
The foreigners fade away,
And come frightened from their hideouts.
The LORD lives!
Blessed be my Rock!
Let the God of my salvation be exalted.
It is God who avenges me,
And subdues the peoples under me;
He delivers me from my enemies.
You also lift me up above those who rise against me;
You have delivered me from the violent man.
Therefore I will give thanks to You, O LORD, among the Gentiles,

And sing praises to Your name.
Great deliverance He gives to His king,
And shows mercy to His anointed,
To David and his descendants forevermore" (NKJV).

Wow. With a lump in my throat, I sat in my chair in that upstairs guest bedroom, begging God to show me what to do next. And He did. I knew without a doubt that I was to confront my husband that very night. After dinner, our family decided to watch *The Lion, The Witch, and the Wardrobe*[12] together. As we watched the movie, I continued praying and asking God for strength, and for Him to open the door and tell me when to speak. By the end of the movie, my husband had fallen asleep as he is prone to do. I got up and started to do the dishes, all too eager to use this nap as my excuse to put off the dreaded conversation till another day. While I was standing in front of the sink, I heard the Lord say, ***"Go."*** He told me my husband would be just awakened from his sleep upon my confronting him, and therefore startled, not having the wherewithal to conjure a lie. I put the children to bed and followed this plan.

Upon being awakened and confronted, my husband immediately admitted to being unfaithful to me. Because of what God had been lovingly showing me over the past year, however, I began by telling my husband that I was not going to leave him, but that I knew he was committing adultery. After confirming my accusation, he asked me how I knew. I told him God had shown me the truth in the Bible. He seemed baffled by my reply. No doubt, this was because I had confronted him numerous times before; but he always had a story, and we never arrived at the truth. He then asked me where God had shown me this evidence, and I gave him the passage—Psalm 50. He said it scared him to know that God could just tell me that, with no other evidence presently against him. I began to ask more questions. He said he was not ready to discuss any of it. At that moment, I didn't think any more or even consult with God. In my pain, I told my husband if he was not willing to talk to me, he needed to leave.

The verse featured at the beginning of this chapter is the one the Lord gave to my dad the morning he began praying for our family, immediately after I told him our news. None of us knew how long this all would last.

But the Lord knew. And he told my daddy, ""For I," says the LORD," will be a wall of fire all around her, and I will be the glory in her midst""" (angel speaking for God, Zechariah 2:5).

And He *would be*.

CHAPTER 10

"Therefore I say to you, do not worry about your life, what you will eat; nor about the body, what you will put on. Life is more than food and the body is more than clothing. Consider the ravens, for they neither sow nor reap, which have neither storehouse nor barn; and God feeds them. Of how much more value are you than the birds? And which of you by worrying can add one cubit to his stature? If you then are not able to do the least, why are you anxious for the rest? Consider the lilies, how they grow: they neither toil nor spin; and yet I say to you, even Solomon in all his glory was not arrayed like one of these. If then God so clothes the grass, which today is in the field and tomorrow is thrown into the oven, how much more will He clothe you, O you of little faith? And do not seek what you should eat or what you should drink, nor have an anxious mind. For all these things the nations of the world seek after, and your Father knows that you need these things. But seek the kingdom of God, and all these things shall be added to you. Do not fear, little flock, for it is your Father's good pleasure to give you the kingdom."

~ Luke 12:22-32

My husband left our family on November 8, 2008. I had no idea where he was going, but I suspected he would stay with his sister or with his best friend. I was to learn later that he went to live with this other woman for the next several months. When he left, I couldn't decide if I was elated or in despair. The immediate relief from his presence was liberating. When he was in our home, there was no peace, but such a spirit of tension and unrest. We were not loving each other, but only tolerating each other—and that for years. The freedom and strength I felt after having heard and obeyed God's voice confidently and in truth that night was palpable. The children were asleep by this time, so I spent the next few hours praising God and thanking Him that this lie was finally unearthed, and also pondering what would come next.

I also called Tracy, the Soul Sister who was still living in Seattle at the time. Her husband, a youth pastor in those days, answered the phone and told me she was out of town visiting her family. He stayed on the phone with me for about an hour, while I conveyed God's revelation and the events that followed. He shared a story with me about two of his family members whose lives were almost destroyed by adultery, but the wife chose to forgive her husband. At one point, the wife said that the bitterness she allowed her heart to feel for so long was actually more painful than the adultery committed against her. I was so grateful for this encouraging word, all the while realizing I was probably in for a long road ahead. Little did I know how long. I felt such a peace that night, though. I knew I was in my Savior's arms, and that I could just rest there. I slept well that night with those arms wrapped around me.

As I learned more about our situation, I discovered that my husband had been in this affair for a little over four years, or since our son was about 1 ½ years old. Interestingly, discerning from my journals, this is exactly the time the Lord began waking me up day after day, at 4:30 a.m., to pray. Sometimes I obeyed. Sometimes I went back to sleep. Incidentally, I also found an instance in my journal, written right about that same time frame, regarding a big hairy fight between my husband and me. My father had come over to try to diffuse the situation, after I had packed my bags and decided I was leaving and my husband had taken my keys. Consequently, this was the exact time in our marriage that our finances became extremely dicey. Oh, how I wish I would have been more diligent in obedience and in prayer during those days! I had no idea, but God did. Clearly, God wanted me to be sober and vigilant. Only He knew what was to come.

I wanted to leave. I wanted to run. I wanted to cry. I wanted to scream.

Unveiled

Most of all, I wanted to divorce my husband. I did cry. Lots and lots of crying. Some screaming too. Some fist-pounding. I wanted to die, but I knew I had to protect my babies. Then, I remembered the way I had felt when I had committed adultery in my first marriage—the shame I had felt when the full-on emotional abuse had begun setting in, dealt by the man I had left my husband for. That was worse than this. Honestly. This was a cake walk, compared to the shame I had felt when I had destroyed my own marriage and latched on to someone who did not know my worth or value. And, as time wore on, I began to understand that there was a much bigger picture to this puzzle than the individual pieces I could see in front of me now.

I remember standing at the back door of our house, just days after my husband had left, asking God why I had to go through this. I heard the words in my spirit so clearly at that moment, ***"This is for MY glory."*** And as time wore on, I could actually see how God was truly working all things together for HIS glory. You see, had I not fallen so hard in my first marriage, I may not have obeyed God's voice when He began speaking His will for my life now, as I was experiencing the other side of the same coin. I was walking down the very road upon which I had laid the gravel in the beginning, with my hateful thoughts and actions and lies. Now it was my turn. But ironically God was saying, ***"No, this time you will not handle it like you want to … you will handle it the way I want you to. You will not turn and run. You will face the music. And you will do it with grace and dignity and by My Spirit. And you will watch Me work miracles of healing in all of your lives."***

Well, the grace and dignity was definitely not a given. But God's Spirit overcame my flesh more often than not. One day, while sitting at the kitchen table, I heard God speak to me again in my spirit. He said, ***"Rebuke what you see with your own eyes."*** Then He took me to 2 Corinthians 4:17-18 which explains, "For our light affliction, which is but for a moment, is working for us a far more exceeding *and* eternal weight of glory, while we do not look at the things which are seen, but at the things which are not seen. For the things which are seen *are* temporary, but the things which are not seen *are* eternal."

What a great reminder. The only way I could do this faith walk in any capacity was to *believe God* for the things He was telling me and the promises He had given and would keep on giving me. Looking at the earthly fear-producing distractions from the enemy would never help me to accomplish any God-given goal or realize the promises He said would come to pass.

God gave me over and over again the passages about the lying (false) prophets (Ezekiel 13, Micah 2:10-11, Jeremiah 27-28). Sadly, some of the people I turned to for advice in the beginning were the most surprising. God had given me some very specific truths about things to stay away from and ways He wanted me to purify our home; but I was met with distrust and disobedience to the Holy Spirit, as more than one friend conveyed their "opinion" of our situation.

I would learn that these passages about the lying prophets were also warnings for me and admonitions about ways to pray for my husband during this time. Clearly there were many "false prophets" in his world—people giving him advice about our situation who really had no business doing so. There were so many of those "friends" in his life who would hear his story and then give him a false sense of peace about what he was doing, like he wasn't actually wrecking everything he held dear, his own world included.

Some days I felt physically sick from the spiritual heaviness of everything the Lord was showing me and telling me to pray about, and Satan's response in the form of physical attacks on my person. I was fasting often, as the Lord led, and rebuking these false prophets—along with everything else God told me to rebuke—in Jesus' name. I was in a total, all-out war with the enemy that did not let up, even sometimes in my sleep and dreams. God was my ONLY protector and provider during those days, which turned into years.

God gave me passage after passage of scripture, after sermon message, after spoken word, after dream, *etc.* to let me know that in no way, shape, or form was I to leave my marriage. We were married for life, and only He knew how to heal it—which He would absolutely do if I would let Him. But I had to surrender. Luke 16:18, Luke 17:3-4, 2 Corinthians 10:3-5, 2 Corinthians 11:2, Isaiah 60-62, Joel 2, Isaiah 57:17-19, John 21:22, 2 Corinthians 3:8, Zephaniah 3:17, I Corinthians 2:9, Jeremiah 29:11, Isaiah 43, Isaiah 58, Isaiah 54:4-7, Isaiah 54:13 & 17, Isaiah 55:11-56:1-2, Psalm

34-37, Psalm 27, 2 Chronicles 20, Joshua 10:27-43, Joshua 11:9 & 15, Deuteronomy 28:1-12, and on and on and on.

Every day He spoke healing messages of His power and His love for me, and that I was to stay in this fight that only HE could share and only HE could win. I had to let Him do it, or I was toast. We all were. I had no choice but to surrender my will to the King of Kings and the Lord of Lords who was my everything, my all in all. And I knew what it meant to disobey. I had been down that road before. It was a long, hard, dark and lonely road with no one to guide me but me. I was not down for that again. I knew if I obeyed my Creator that He would not steer me wrong. Not now, and not ever. I was finally learning that lesson in its truest form. I would declare HIS praise! My very life and the lives of my children depended on Him.

On November 15, the day I had set aside to plant the rest of the wheat, I remember standing at the bar that divided our kitchen from our family room. Head bowed and a knot in my stomach, I asked the Lord once again to please heal my family. I heard His words, clear as a bell, in my heart. He said, **"It is already done."**

> Journal entry November 19, 2008 (as I continued to process this message from the Lord about the wheat):
>
> "Maybe what He's saying to me is to plant the seeds from my life and use this as a testimony. Plant seeds for the harvest in other people's lives and in my family. Please speak to me, Lord."

I would like to say that the next few days and months, and then years were full of peace and joy for me. That would be a bit of an exaggeration. Parts of the next four years were absolute destruction for sure. And I had no idea when I began this journey, how long the duration would actually be. How could I? There was no way to see the future. But, during that time, I grew immensely close to my Lord. He was my every breath, my waking and my sleeping, my food and my sustenance, my day and my night. I began to understand during that time what the term "Living Water" truly means. I was in the Word day and night. The Lord had already taught me how to fast and pray several years before, and during this time it became my biggest weapon against the enemy.

I was not working when my husband left, so some days I would literally sit in my chair in my quiet time room and cry and pray and read God's Word all day. When He told me to fast, I would fast. I learned so much about His Holy Spirit during this time. I grew deeper and deeper with God, and trusted my every move to His leading. I learned to hear God's voice through prayer and sitting quietly with Him and through His holy Word. He would often take me to places in the Bible that referenced fasting. I learned during that time to ask my Heavenly Father "how long?" and "what kind of fast?" Through continued prayer and being in His Word, the Holy Spirit would show me the duration and type of my fast. Sometimes it was for three days with no food or water—sometimes just 24 hours or just until dinner. But I learned to be in tune with God so that I could be obedient to His will. God literally worked miracle upon miracle directly as a result of my fasting and pressing in to Him in prayer.

There was so much back and forth in the beginning. Neither my husband nor I knew exactly what this was to look like, so there was often confusion as we decided whether to live together or apart as we worked on things. And truthfully, I was the only one of us who consistently knew that we were actually working on anything, and that only because of the Lord's faithfulness to continually remind me. Often things erupted into violence when my husband and I were together for long enough periods of time. I was painfully struggling with my heart toward him, as he was not exactly immediately repentant. Oh, a few times he said the right things. But his heart was in a war with the enemy, and he was continuing to be knocked down and to act defensively toward me. Even though the Lord continued to teach and prepare me for this, I was also often knocked into left field as a result of my own anger. Amazingly enough, God continued to speak His tender mercies to me in the middle of the night, often waking me up singing. He never left my side.

Thankfully, the senior pastor from our home church agreed to see us on a semi-regular basis. He was an extremely busy man, so we were thankful for the time he allotted us. I knew my husband truly respected him, and I was grateful to God for this blessing. The first time we met with him, he did not pull any punches. He made sure in no uncertain terms that my husband understood that he was responsible under God for the healing of our family, and that he was to be proactive about doing his part to get us on the road to recovery. Our pastor then gave us a plan to spend time together as a family on weekends, while still living separately for the majority of the time. We planned to spend Christmas together that year, at our pastor's leading. He also connected us with a mentoring couple who had been in a similar situation and could walk with us in the day-to-day of this nitty-gritty minefield. We were grateful to God to say the least.

Sadly, though, sooner than later this too came to an end. There was too much water under the bridge at this point for things to go smoothly or exactly as planned. My husband didn't believe the couple was suited for us, or really for *him*. He was in a defensive place, and any little error in judgement set him off during that time. And the Lord continued to show me *adultery* in His Word, letting me know we were definitely not out of the woods yet. Though I wanted to believe we were on a fast track to healing, as God would have it, we were in for the long haul. Nonetheless, I continued to offer God my sacrifices of praise on a daily basis. He continued to be my all in all.

CHAPTER 11

"Most assuredly, I say to you, unless a grain of wheat falls into the ground and dies, it remains alone; but if it dies, it produces much grain."

~ John 12:24

On December 30, 2008 God rescued our home from foreclosure. We owed five months of payments: over $5,300. We were set to begin foreclosure proceedings on January 2nd. The woman on the phone told me a day or so before that the hardship we applied for would take at least a week, maybe two, to process. We didn't have that long. She said there was nothing she could do. Next thing I know, we got a phone call saying our application was approved. They had moved all of the five months of payments we owed—ten payments in all—to the back of the note, and moved our next payment to one month away. Just. Like. That. God had been telling me since July 2007 that we would not lose our home. Several well-meaning friends had suggested at this point that we sell our home and move to something we could better afford. But God said no. He told me in 2 Samuel 7:10 that year that this was our home, and that we would not have to move. And I believed Him.

A new friend told me during this time, "There is only one truth. You have to walk in that light; and eventually your feelings will follow." (Incidentally, this friend had suffered bout after bout of epileptic seizures—one grand mal seizure and then eight other seizures in one day—ravaging her brain to the point where she now had the memory recall of a fifth grader.) I was discovering that my feelings were NOT to be followed. They were dangerous and misleading—*real*, but dangerous. I could only trust

God to show me His truth. I asked Him during these dark days to please turn me into the woman, the wife, the mommie HE wanted me to be. Only He could do that.

I also began to pray that the Lord would not allow the generational curse of adultery to be passed on to our children, or the curses of fornication, anger, fear, anxiety, pride, depression, insecurity, bitterness, unforgiveness, critical nature, lewdness or drunkenness. And GOD gave me a promise! Right after I prayed that prayer for the first time, He gave me Isaiah 61:4 which says, "And they shall rebuild the old ruins, they shall raise up the former desolations; and they shall repair the ruined cities, the desolations of many generations." WOW. Then Isaiah 58:12, "Those from among you shall build the old waste places; you shall raise up the foundations of many generations; and you shall be called the Repairer of the Breach; the Restorer of Streets to Dwell in."

I asked the Lord to help me give back to those who had given me so much. When He began providing those opportunities, I was elated. It felt so good to be giving again! I had been taking and taking, and just really in the position of <u>needing</u>—and having to learn to be humble about it all. This, too, was important for me to learn. Without the gifts from so many—gifts of time, friendship, money, groceries, gift cards, a year's worth of dinners, brand-new dishes, paying our bills, paying for me to get my hair done (!), rides to and from school, etc., I would not have seen so much of the goodness of our God. Countless friends, old and new, became the Lord's hands and feet to our family during our desperate time of need.

In January of 2009, my husband informed me that I needed to get a job. Not having worked in over six years, the mere thought was daunting to me. And then there were the specifics. I knew I couldn't go back to doing what I knew. My heart wasn't even in that world of fashion and glamour anymore. Now my heart was with these beautiful babies God had given me. I was their world and they were mine. I couldn't bear the thought of leaving them for someone else to raise. The thought of daycare made me nauseous. It didn't take long for me to figure out my path for work. Huddled by the kitchen phone one afternoon, I looked up local daycares/preschools. I saw a page that caught my eye, and I dialed the number. Yes, they were looking for workers. Yes, I should come interview right away. Not what I wanted to hear, but I made the appointment anyway. After a brief interview at the daycare, I came home. Soon the phone call came, and I was hired. Uggghhh. Upon hanging up the phone, I fell to the floor sobbing. So, this was it. I was officially a working mom.

By the time I began working again, my husband was no longer living in our home, even under the part-time arrangement our pastor had put in place. Out of the blue one day, during those first weeks of my new job, our two-year old baby girl began saying to me, "It <u>won't</u> shake," to which I finally replied one night, "You're right, baby, it <u>won't</u> <u>shake</u>. The enemy <u>cannot</u> shake our family. We are the Lord's family. He is hedging us in front and behind." I just told the Lord I loved Him so much, over and over. He *was* our righteousness.

Working at this preschool/daycare was truly not at all what I had imagined. I cannot begin to describe accurately the blessings God had in store for me in this next installment of my life. Our daughter was placed in a 2-year old class, and made wonderful new friends. Two of those friends have remained her closest friends to this day, and their mamas are some of my best friends in the world. I took a floater position at the daycare, so I was literally free during most of my day to go from classroom to classroom where there was a need or where I wanted to be. This afforded me the opportunity to be with my daughter at several intervals throughout the day, and many times at lunch. My son came and stayed there after school (my dear friend dropped him off each day) and made several friends as well. His school was right around the corner—I could even walk there during lunch if I wanted to. And the food was free! Breakfast and lunch and tuition were free for workers and children. I began to love going to work in the morning. It was the craziest thing. I was up at 5 a.m. and in a good mood, as I drank my coffee and prepared for my day.

I drove a bus in the morning at the daycare, taking children to school whose parents dropped them there early. I had many opportunities to witness and share the love of Christ with these kids, who came from all walks of life. Often God would highlight certain children or situations, so that He could minister to many in need through me. Because I drove the bus, I had the freedom to talk with the children to and from school each day. I had the privilege of leading several to Christ, along with many opportunities to pour into them and speak what the Holy Spirit would daily lay on my heart. Because I was a floater and worked in the back with the older kids in the afternoon, I was able to minister to many of them in a personal way. Often God would just point out special students He knew were hurting and give me words to say to let them know they were seen by Him, and that they were not alone.

Journal entry February 14, 2009 (Valentine's Day):

"Yesterday I fasted. I was asking God to bring T home last night, or this weekend. But I was also praising Him and continuing to ask Him to change me, change my thoughts, give me patience and self-control, help me to be a better wife and mom, servant, etc. This morning at work, I met (we will call him 'Jamal'). I am now on the a.m. van run. He rides to school from (daycare). He was angry, having a problem with another kid and saying he wished he could put him in jail. He was disrespectful to (teacher) and to me. But I talked to him about Jesus and about making Him happy, and about how being kind and loving when someone else is ugly to you is actually more powerful than being ugly right back. He had a pretty negative response—no big surprise. I asked him if he knew Jesus. He said no. I saw him again in the afternoon in the playroom—he was passing through while I was doing a potty break for (teacher). I asked him if he wanted me to tell him how he could get to know Jesus. He said yes. His eyes were sad and lonely. I told him Jesus was God—God's Son—and began to explain the plan of salvation to him. His eyes filled with tears as he listened. When I was finished, we moved to a room in the clubhouse where we could have some privacy. I prayed that God would give us some time alone and uninterrupted. He did. Jamal asked Jesus to come into his heart yesterday. I told him I would bring him a Bible this next week. He said his mom and dad didn't know Jesus, but that his grandmother did. I told him to call her and tell her what he had done and to tell his parents."

I worked a nap room for two hours a day after my two-hour lunch. I almost always brought my Bible and spent the time talking to God and reading His Word. He constantly spoke to me then, as at other times, giving me certain passages over and over (Jeremiah 32:17, 37-43 was one of the first places He took me) to remind me of His promises of healing to me and for my marriage and family. I drew nearer to Him by the day. I ate, breathed, and slept in the bosom of my Savior, taking every waking thought to Him.

And the women. The hurting women. They came in droves as God brought them to me and allowed me to share my story, which was truly only the story of His grace, mercy and abundant love in the midst of a catastrophic storm that threatened to take the very life of my family. Many of these women were in deep anguish. There was so much pain represented in so many who were working alongside me. But, one by one, God gave me opportunities to minister to each one in need, as He carved out time for us to talk and to get to know each other—on the playground, in an after-school movie room, in nap rooms, serving breakfast to children before driving the buses. He was using my life and my pain for His glory there on a daily basis.

One day, about a month after I began working, I met a woman. We will call her "Sheila." She was a floater like me, and we were working in the same nap room one afternoon. Not long after we began talking, Sheila started to share why she was working there. Her husband had been unfaithful and had left their family, and their house was in foreclosure. Sheila enrolled her two children in daycare and afterschool care, and worked as a teacher, just like me. Her children were around the same ages as mine, and her daughter was in my daughter's class. She was a Christian. She was very angry at her husband, and was headed for divorce. I began to share with her what God had spoken to me, and the radical path toward healing that He had us on. She was listening. She was fuming still and vacillating between the numbness and the fury toward her husband. But she was listening. God allowed our hearts to connect that day, and for many years to come. Through the weeks and months to come, Sheila was practically my lifeline at this daycare center. Just having someone with me every day who knew and understood my plight and was in the same fight against the enemy was like a bulwark to my soul. We were often in the same classrooms and sometimes took lunch together. Just seeing her each day gave me strength in the Lord. We were both also bus drivers, which meant we got to see each other in the early mornings, and catch up while we served breakfast. God was at work all over the place.

In February, I went to the county courthouse to file a restraining order on the woman my husband was having an affair with. Even after my husband had left our home, she had continued to harass my family with phone calls. She had shown so much gall with her attempts to frighten us—I did not want to take any chances, now that we were separated. I did not have the money for an attorney, so I went to the courthouse library and learned how to file the restraining order myself. On February 16, 2009, I went to court for my hearing. The night before, God had given me Joel 2:25 again, affirming to me that He would restore to me the years the locusts had eaten. I arrived at the courthouse the next morning ready to do battle, my dad and a good friend at my side. The other woman didn't even show up. Praying and choking back some tears, I told the judge my story on my own. He granted my request immediately. Legally now, this woman could not come near my children's school, my work or our home for two years.

My husband lost yet another job on the day of this hearing. He left with one paycheck and the promise of another in a couple of weeks. I also got paid: my check was $423, and the electric bill was $305. The mentor from our church that I was still walking with advised me not to put my paycheck into our joint account at this time, as it was pretty clear my husband was not currently engaged in this marriage. I followed her advice and trusted God with the rest. He was continuing to show me, day by day, that I could trust Him with every single detail of my life. And that He loved me more than I could comprehend.

The following Sunday I visited a local church with a friend and her family. The pastor showed a video of a woman who puts up Christmas trees for chemo patients. She said she had this ministry because she had cancer and went through chemo herself. I heard the Lord saying, ***"That is what***

I have for you with these women." His words were as clear as a bell in my heart. I wept and wept. I was falling so deeply in love with my Adonai.

The next weekend was a fun, girly weekend, just our daughter and me, as our son was in El Paso at a wrestling tournament with his dad. Saturday night it came over me like a wave. I felt the Lord's peace, His love, His strength, His truth about myself and about my husband's sin. I said it aloud, "Today is the day—February 21st—I will no longer be oppressed or depressed or in despair." I was beginning to truly know who I was, *who I am*, in Christ Jesus.

At our next counseling appointment, our pastor again enforced my husband's role as the head of our family and explained that the wife was made to mirror or reflect what she received from her head. He stressed the importance of my husband taking responsibility for the healing of our marriage. He then asked him when he could come home on a full-time basis. My husband said he could have done it the day before. Our pastor then asked him when he *would* come home. He answered that he would come home the following weekend. Our pastor told my husband that if he would trust him, we would begin to have a new marriage inside 90 days. I knew then that my husband's heart was still hard and cold. He was still trying to blame me for most of what had happened, and to argue about truly taking responsibility for our healing. But he said he would come home. I trusted the Lord to heal him, and to heal *us*. I was just going to try and stay out of the way and to let God do all the work. Easier said than done.

Four days later, I awoke from a dream in which I was welcoming my husband back into my arms intimately. I felt so much sadness upon awakening. I just cried and cried until I fell back to sleep. But I wrote in my journal on that day, "I just have to trust the Lord. He knows the way that I take; and when He has tested me, I shall come forth as pure gold" (Job 23:10).

Once I even prayed out loud, "Lord, please help me to love my husband as Hosea loved the prostitute." I remember being bowed down near the bathtub in our master bathroom at the time. I can tell you, this prayer did not emanate from my own head. That prayer was most definitely the prayer of the Holy Spirit in and through my soul. In fact, I kind of jumped aside, after the words came out, in a Groucho Marx puppet master kind of way, as if to say, "What? I definitely did NOT mean to pray THAT prayer!" But the Lord knew. He knew He prayed it through me, and He knew it was His will for my life. I would obey.

March 6, 2009 my husband came home to live with our family. God instructed a sweet friend to call me the night before. Actually, she was just returning my call—funny how God works. She told me to just be as kind as possible, and to make our home inviting for him. Our pastor's executive assistant also prayed for us the week before and told me to not continue to bring the affair up. It was truly incredible how God sent His messengers all along the way to help me hear Him. Our first night back together as a family was wonderful. I made a steak, baked potato, and salad dinner complete with red wine. We ate on the fine china, and I rented two movies for us for the weekend. We had a great time with the kids and got along well. We laughed and joked and talked to each other lovingly.

The Lord had given me so much Scripture to guide me in this process and prepare me for what was to come. He encouraged me with Isaiah 60-61, John 12:24 & 32, Joel 2:21-32, Isaiah 43, Isaiah 57 & 58, Isaiah 52:12. He even gave me the story of *The Little Red Hen*[13] several times, some while reading to our son. The Lord continued speaking to me about the wheat, telling me that a grain of wheat remained alone *unless* it fell to the ground and died. Then and only then did it produce much grain.

Journal entry March 12, 2009:

"Two days ago, God worked another miracle. I have been praying for Jamal's mommie to accept Jesus as her Savior. On Tuesday, she found me in a class and asked me to come see her later. When I finally did, at the end of the day, she told me she had a terrible weekend, but that at one point she left to take a walk and just asked God to 'give me a sign.' She said she heard, clear as day, 'Ms. Catherine.' I was floored and told her that the Lord had been laying her on my heart too, and that I had prayed for another opportunity to talk to her, after she told me they were all Christians because they 'went to church every Sunday.'

She prayed to accept Christ right in her classroom that day. I have never seen a more eager or willing heart. Parents were coming in to get their children, and she did not care. She wanted to keep praying. Yesterday, we had the opportunity to talk for about an hour because I took her to Walmart to get her car. We shared our testimonies, which were very similar. What a blessing. It's funny—yesterday was the 2nd day of a 2-day fast God told me to begin. Now I know why. T also came to me night before last and asked me what was the best time for us to pray together. I almost fell out of bed. But that morning, I had asked God for an open door to bring up praying together again."

Wow, God. Just WOW.

CHAPTER 12

"How beautiful upon the mountains are the feet of him who brings good news, who proclaims peace, who brings glad tidings of good things, who proclaims salvation, who says to Zion, 'Your God reigns!'"

~ Isaiah 52:7

God never ceased speaking to me. One weekend, not long after my husband came home that first time, we began getting incessant phone calls from a Georgia number. They started on Friday and were really ramping up by Saturday. By this time, I had learned that the adulteress' family lived there, so, I was on high alert. Once when I picked up, the person hung up on me. My husband and I got into a big fight about the whole thing. I ended up calling the police after my husband left to coach wrestling practice, thinking that because of this new temporary restraining order this woman could now be sent to jail for harassing me and my family. The officer came and took all my info. I was crying and visibly upset. The phone rang again while she was there, and it was the same GA number. The officer asked if she could answer it. She did. The caller was from our mortgage company. The officer told me when she hung up the phone that sometimes God used these situations to test us. When I began crying again, she asked if she could give me a hug. I asked her if she was a Christian. She said she was. She asked me if I had seen the movie *Fireproof*,[14] and then told me I should buy the book *The Love Dare*.[15] (The "dare" is a 30-day trial in which the reader follows instructions to love their partner tangibly, and so begins the healing in their marriage.) I immediately said, "You want me to do it?" She nodded yes. I knew the right answer. She spoke to me about forgiveness, and how I was supposed to forgive my husband 70 X 7. She gave an example of her friend's marriage, and how God put it back together. I hugged her and told her she had gone above and beyond the call of duty, and that God had used her in a mighty way that day. She told me I could call her at any time; and she would make a courtesy call to my house to check on me. I was then and am now constantly amazed at the God I serve. He is truly everywhere.

Sadly, my children were very aware and affected by all of our family's trials. It is very hard, if not impossible, to hide that stuff. One day on our way home from work, our daughter said to me for no reason in particular, "You're happy, Mommie! You're happy. You're…not sad, Mommie; you're happy!" (in her little cherub way). I was in disbelief. She actually remembered when her daddy was gone, and that I was sad then. I do remember her saying one day, while he was gone and I was particularly moody and upset, "You're sad, Mommie?" And now she could tell the difference. Oh, the roller coaster their little hearts were both on.

I remember praying once during that time with a dear friend. She prayed one day that my husband would see me and know that his wife was "the real deal." It was amazing. Right when she prayed those words, I felt the awesome power of the Holy Spirit. It was like a strong bolt or charge of peaceful and comforting energy. I knew His arms were all around me and that *He was going to do this*. The angel of the Lord was encamped all around me. And He delivered me (Psalm 34:7).

Journal entry April 16, 2009:

"Last night I totally lost it with T. He was being a little rude to me, because he was tired, and I just lost my cool. I kept thinking about him and that evil woman and how they were completely shacked up together. He was playing daddy with her and her kids, and his kids were home missing him. It made me so angry I could just have punched him. Instead I just yelled and cried and went upstairs. Then I came down and I told him to go upstairs. I apologized this morning, but I am just still having a really hard time with this. He prayed with me this morning and told me how sorry he was. God's miraculous healing will be <u>all</u> that can make this hurt go away. Incidentally, T needs to be hurt as badly or worse than I am hurting. He doesn't even understand the magnitude of damage he has done to himself with his own sin. I really wish I could go and see that woman and ruin her life. I wish I could call her mother and tell her what her daughter is doing. I wish I could tell her children that their 'Uncle T' is <u>my</u> husband and he has his own children. I wish I could get her fired from her job. I would love to see her homeless on the street, penniless, without a rock for a pillow. I know It's wrong to sit around and wish bad things on others, but I do take comfort in knowing that the Lord, <u>my</u> God, will take care of me and will exact His vengeance on my enemies. It's not my job. Please help me, Lord, to be loving and forgiving to my husband. Please help me to forgive his family for leaving me out in the cold. Please help me to someday forgive this woman. Please help me to get my permanent restraining order on the 27th. Give me the words to say to represent myself, and give me the evidence I need. Calm my nerves, Lord. Help me to be at peace. Please make my husband stand up for his wife and come to court with me. Please heal my completely broken heart, Jesus. Please take away this ache inside my soul. Please give me the oil of joy for my mourning and beauty for my ashes (Isaiah 61:3).

I feel constantly like there are tears right behind my eyes, just waiting to come out."*

Journal entry April 28, 2009:

"Yesterday I represented myself in the final trial for the permanent restraining order against (the adulteress). It was miraculously awesome. The Lord, my God, was so completely with me. His angels were encamped all around me. And *He delivered me*. I did not fumble my words. I did not cry. I was nervous, and it showed, but I was also respectful and eloquent in court. I was unaware that I had to file the order with the court before the trial. The judge granted my permanent restraining order anyway, pending the form being filed. I went with bells on to the legal library and filed the order. The judge will sign it today or tomorrow. I could not stop singing and praising the Lord yesterday.

Father, *please* help *me* to be the wife You have created me to be. Humble, serving, respectful, loving, honoring my husband, submissive to You by submitting to him, faithful, kind, good, gentle, patient, forgiving, nurturing, caring for him, sacrificing, exhibiting self-control at all times with joy and peace in my heart. Help me to be chaste, wise, discreet and a good steward of all that you give me. Help me to be generous to all.

Father, please help T to be the spiritual leader of our family that You have created him to be. Bring men around him to sharpen him and hold him accountable, as iron sharpens iron. Please give him someone, at least one, who understands spiritual warfare completely and who is mature and astute in Your Word, Lord, and who is a great steward and who is a good teacher in this area and who is strong in You, Lord, and will not back down to him. The only person who has not backed down to T so far on some level is (our senior pastor who counseled us). Lord, You know my husband is very persuasive. Give him a man, at least one, who will not be swayed by him. Help him to re-establish the relationship with (the mentoring husband from the couple at church) or please give us another couple to counsel us—or maybe just a more regular counselor, Lord. I'm beginning to think that is Your will at this time. Please help him to love me, cherish me, desire me, pursue me and romance me—I guess those last 2 are the same. Please help him to seek You, Lord, and Your righteousness, to seek first the kingdom of heaven and all these things shall be added unto him. Help him to know You have "shown (him), oh man, what is good and what (the Lord requires of him is) to do justly, to love mercy and to walk humbly with (his) God" (Micah 6:8). Help him to be a good steward of everything You have given him. Help us to stick to our budget together once our money isn't so funny anymore. Help him to hunger and thirst for righteousness and for Your Word. Help him to be full of grace, mercy, love and forgiveness. Help him to be his family's protector—our shield from any and all danger, whether it be people, places, things or spiritual elements. Help him to be our number one provider. And, please Father, bring me home from work. I don't want to work anymore. I want to be home taking care of my family and nurturing them and managing my home. Please help me to do a more joyful, peaceful job of that when it is time again. Help T to repent of the things in his life that don't please You. Help him to fall head over heels in <u>love</u> with You, Jesus, and never again place any other gods before You. Help me to do that, too. Give him a broken spirit and a broken and contrite heart (Psalm 51:17). Strip him of all his defenses and strip me of mine. Give *me* a broken and contrite heart and a broken spirit. Break us both free from the stronghold of pride, in Jesus' name. Help us not to gossip or slander anyone, especially each other, or each other's parents. Make him kind, good, gentle, <u>faithful</u>, forgiving, patient, loving, self-controlled, full of joy and peace. Never allow him to look at another woman again in a lustful or indecent way without being repulsed. Break our hearts with what breaks Your heart. Make us to be on <u>fire</u> for You, Lord, witnessing to others and not backing away from the precious chance to lead someone to Jesus. Give him a bond with my father one day, Lord. Help him to see my dad through Your eyes, and himself through Your eyes. Help me to see his parents through Your eyes and myself through Jesus' eyes. Help T and I to see *each other* through Your eyes. Cover our home with Your protective blanket of peace, love, and joy. I love You, Lord and I trust You for *all* of this. I know You can and will do this.

In Jesus' name, amen."

Journal entry August 29, 2009:

"John 11:40 '…Did I not say to you that if you would believe you would see the glory of God?'

Jesus purposely waited in another town 2 days after Lazarus died so that God would be glorified. Mary said (v. 32), 'Lord, if you would have been here, my brother would not have died.'

I remember asking the Lord why it had to be 4 ½ years—why this sin had to be so horrible and go on for so long. I had asked the Lord this question, standing in front of the back door to our home, just days or maybe a couple of weeks after T left. And the Holy Spirit clearly told me, **'This is for My glory.'**

(v. 39) 'Lord, by this time there is a stench, for he has been dead four days.'

(v. 41, 42) 'Father, I thank You that You have heard Me. And I know that You always hear Me, but because of the people who are standing by I said this, that they may believe that You sent Me.'

John 12:3-8. Mary worshipped Jesus with the very costly oil of Spikenard. *She knew the good part.*

Many witnessed Lazarus' resurrection (John 12:40). 'Most assuredly, I say to you, unless a grain of wheat falls into the ground and dies, it remains alone; but if it dies, it produces much grain' (John 12:24).

As I sit and write, I am in the backyard, overlooking the small plot of wheat that T and I symbolically planted. Our marriage had to completely die for us to produce much grain, so that the Lord would be eternally glorified.

John 12:32 'And I (Jesus), if I am lifted up from the earth, will draw all peoples to Myself.'

It is my (our) job to continue lifting Jesus up from the earth in all of this. Continue glorifying His name so that others, even my husband, will be drawn to Him.

Help me, Father, today, to lift Jesus up no matter what. To glorify Your name. To stand still and see the salvation of the Lord which He will accomplish for us <u>today</u> (Exodus 14:13). The Lord will fight for us (me), and I shall hold my peace. Help me to be like Joshua and Caleb who, when spying out a land <u>full</u> of giants, came back glorifying Your name, Lord. Not looking at the obstacles before them, but on the beauty of the land the Lord had promised them. Their eyes remained on You when they had seen the promised land. And they and their descendants <u>alone</u> received their inheritance, because they chose to believe You when everyone else did not."

In September of that year my car was repossessed. A Christian couple came to take it. They couldn't have been sweeter. They told me stories of the Lord's greatness in their own lives and testified that He was probably setting me up for something much better. I knew in my spirit that was true. They were praying for a baby, and I began to pray for God to give them one. God already had our ride situation worked out with kind friends who offered. I didn't even have to ask. My boss also offered to give us rides to school and work while we got things worked out. The following day, my husband's car was repossessed. Six days later, I got my car back when we filed for bankruptcy. Incidentally, my dad paid the $600 for us to even file for bankruptcy—we did not have the money to do it on our own. Funny—at the time it happened, both my husband and my father, independently of one another, noted that this last gesture and acceptance of the same actually helped to heal some old wounds and to bring the two of them closer to one another.

By late October, my husband and I were separated again. Our relationship had begun to spiral downward again for the weeks prior to his departure. Just a few weeks before he left, the Lord began showing me *adultery* repeatedly in His Word. He also had me fasting quite a lot. When things eventually blew up between us, I went to stay with my dad and stepmom for a few days.

Journal entry October 26, 2009:

"Nehemiah 9

Psalm 31

2 Chronicles 20

I went to my house today to return T's earpiece and get some more things. He had changed the locks.

Deuteronomy 28 (v.7)

Isaiah 43

You promised me, Lord, that You would heal my family. You told me on November 7th last year, *'It is already done.'*

I <u>believe</u> You, Lord. You have <u>never</u> let me down. You do not speak at random. Your Word will <u>not</u> return to You void. You <u>promised</u>, Lord. You <u>promised</u>. Everyone is watching, Lord, to see what You will do. Do not let me down now, please. Make Your name great. Your name <u>is</u> great. All glory and power and honor be to <u>my</u> King. My Jehovah Rapha, my great Healer. You are Lord of lords and King of kings. I *will* glorify Your name forevermore. I will be in constant praise and adoration of You, my Heavenly Father, my precious Savior. I *will not* doubt You and I *will not* be afraid.

Psalm 18

Psalm 19:14

Isaiah 41:18-20

Isaiah 42

2 Samuel 5"

A few days later, the Lord told me to go home. He told me to leave my father's house (Genesis 12:1) and go back to my husband. On November 12, my husband moved out again—almost a year to the day from when he had left the first time. The Lord had continued to show me that he was being unfaithful again. This time *I* changed the locks. I was ready to file for divorce, and had already contacted an attorney. But God had me stay in the fight. I did not go through with the filing at that time. I could not continue to be in communion with my Lord without purposefully following His will for my life.

The Lord had given me Luke 11:24-26 several times during those days which says, "When an unclean spirit goes out of a man, he goes through dry places seeking rest; and finding none, he says, 'I will return to my house from which I came.' And when he comes, he finds *it* swept and put in order. Then he goes and takes with *him* seven other spirits more wicked than himself, and they enter and dwell there; and the last *state* of that man is worse than the first." (Jesus speaking here.) He was showing me the state of my husband's heart during that time. The enemy was wreaking havoc on his soul.

Meanwhile, I was having my own battle with anger. I prayed often for God to "break up my fallow ground" (Hosea 10:12, Jeremiah 4:3) and to break me free from the prison of anger and unforgiveness. Again, God specifically gave me the story of Paul and Silas praying and singing hymns to God in prison. The prisoners with Paul and Silas there in the jail were listening to them singing as well. Suddenly there was a great earthquake so that the foundations of the prison were shaken, and immediately all the doors were opened and everyone's chains were loosed. And the *jailer* asked Paul and Silas what he must do to be saved! And he was saved and baptized that *very night*. He and his entire family (Acts 16:16-40). What an incredible reminder. The sacrifice of praise is so precious to our God. He knows what we are going through at any and all times. He is not a stranger to our pain, and He is not surprised by anything going on in our world around us. He has allowed our circumstances for His own specific reasons, *always* for our growth, and most of all for His glory—if we will give each situation to Him and let Him make beauty from our ashes. He will do it. He will glorify His name forever through the testimony of His saints. We never know who is watching us in our personal battles.

The Bible says "since we are surrounded by so great a cloud of witnesses, let us lay aside every weight, and the sin which so easily ensnares *us*, and let us run with endurance the race that is set before us, looking unto Jesus, the author and finisher of *our* faith, who for the joy that was set before Him endured the cross, despising the shame, and has sat down at the right hand of the throne of God" (Hebrews 12:1-2). Wow. I don't know about you, but I don't even compare to Jesus in my righteousness, or in any other category. If Jesus could go to the cross for me, having already counted its cost and also having weighed that cost against the glory of God, knowing that the *glory of God wins every time*, surely, I can take up my cross on a daily basis and lay down my life for Him. He gave *all* for me. All means *all*. I fall so short in what I give back to Him on a daily basis. I was asking God to make me holy, as He was holy. And to let my life be a sacrifice of praise to Him alone.

And God continued to speak the word ***"Zerubbabel"*** to me.

Not long after that, my husband took my car. I prayed and asked the

Father to please just "drop one in my lap." Two days later, on November 15th, He did. I came home and there was a check from another one of my Soul Sisters—let's call her "Lucy"—for $200. Then my biological sister just loaned me her car indefinitely, without me asking. I agreed to pay the cheapest of her two car payments. I was overwhelmed. Another month, Lucy paid my entire car payment. God's mercy was and is truly everlasting.

Journal entry November 17th, 2009:

"Three kids got saved on my van yesterday, and one today. We serve a <u>*mighty God*</u>!!!!! One boy (we will call him 'Sam') was baptized over the weekend and was <u>gushing</u> about the experience. He was explaining what it means to be baptized and what it means to be in God's family. I started to try to fill in the holes, but God said, **'Slow down, let him speak.'** Which he *did*—the love of Jesus was just pouring through him. Eventually, together, we explained the plan of salvation. I told the kids I was going to pray, and that if anyone wanted to pray that same prayer in their heart—and if they believed that Jesus was the Son of God, and that He died to save them from their sins—then they could come into God's family that day. One did (we will call him 'Mark')—surprisingly, my biggest trouble maker. I was overjoyed! I loved him up and congratulated him, and we talked about his spiritual birthday and how he was now in God's family and on his way to heaven! Then in a couple of minutes, almost 10, (we will call him 'Nathan') spoke up. 'I want to be in God's family.' So, we prayed and Nathan accepted Jesus in his heart. Next, before we arrived at our last school, (we will call him 'Tucker'), Sam's older brother, spoke up and said he wanted to pray to be in God's family. So, after the rest of the kids got off the van, Tucker asked Jesus to come into <u>his</u> heart. <u>What</u> an amazing morning—and all at the end of a 3-day fast. Wow. I was on <u>fire</u> in my heart! I couldn't stop crying as I called J (dear friend) to tell her the news. She brought up a good point regarding Mark: some of the hardest hearts are the ones who really want God the most. I pray that really is the absolute truth for my T. I pray that Jesus draws him with every breath. I pray he longs for his Savior in such a way that no one, nothing else can compare. Show him, Lord, how to be free from that filthy, empty, lonely, shallow prison he lives in. Show him that the God of the ages is in love with him and is longing for his heart. Show him how much You *adore* him, Lord, and that You will leave the ninety-nine to find his lost heart. Show him who You are, Abba—wonderful, Counselor, mighty GOD, Prince of Peace, Holy One, Jehovah Jireh, Jehovah Rapha, El Elyon, Adonai. Show him what true love is.

Today, before we loaded the vans, (we will call her 'Abigail'), also on my van, said to me, 'I want to pray … for God' (she's five). So, we prayed as soon as we loaded, and Abigail became a member of God's family today. I am amazed and overwhelmed. I am flooded with joy and awe at, and for, my Savior. He is the most excellent friend and miracle worker—above Him there is no other. Truly God most high. It makes me realize, once again, that He still has me here for a reason. Not time to leave yet, as much as I keep asking Him to come home. Or even just if I should get I get a better job. Apparently not, at least not right now. I will wait for You, Lord. I will trust You. Please make me like You, Abba. Patient, peaceful, loving, kind, forgiving, longsuffering, gentle, merciful, joyful. Please put my family back together, Lord. Please heal us.

I Samuel 17-18. God is slaying my enemies for me!

Isaiah 43 & Isaiah 40. God's comfort and promises of healing."

Journal entry November 20th, 2009:

"Luke 15. The prodigal son.

Last night, I was praying and asking the Lord to show me something, <u>anything</u>, to keep me hanging on. I told Him in my flesh everything felt like I was being a big idiot. I turned right here. The first part talks about leaving the 99 sheep in the wilderness to go find that one lost sheep. I know His heart *longs* for T's heart to come home. He is pursuing him and will welcome him with open arms when he finally comes 'to himself.'

Mark 15-16

Jesus <u>died</u> for T too. He died, and He rose again. He can and He will free my husband from this prison he is living in. He can, and He will. I trust Him. LORD, please forgive me for my unbelief. I <u>do</u> believe You. I will wait for You."

Journal entry November 21, 2009:

"Joel 2

Hosea 14, 12-13

Ezekiel 36:23-28 (heart insert)

I felt such peace and deliverance and relief this morning as I read this. I opened right to it, 1st thing right after my fast yesterday. He is continuing to promise me repentance and healing in our family. I just cried and cried.

Joel 2:25

The LORD has spoken to T and to me in a dream saying *'I will restore the years the locust has eaten.'*

Father, please speak to T as the leader of this family. Speak these words to him again, if it is Your will. Show him that *You are GOD* and there is <u>no other.</u> Bring his heart home to You, once and for all. Show him that he is <u>Your</u> child and that You adore him and you will <u>not</u> let him go, but that You hate his sin. Call his wounded heart home to You. In Jesus' precious, strong and mighty name I pray, amen (heart insert)."

Journal entry November 24, 2009:

"Numbers 13-14.

The Israelites are grumbling and saying, 'Why has the Lord brought us to this land, to fall by the sword that our wives and children should become victims?' That's just the point: <u>NO</u>, the LORD has not brought me here for failure. He's brought me here for VICTORY. And just like Joshua and Caleb, I <u>will</u> stand on GOD's promises, on His <u>covenant</u> with me. I will trust <u>Him</u> once and for all and I will do His will. He has had me in this place of just being <u>kind</u> to T and loving him no matter what. It's actually easier than I thought it would be. I just let my Savior do all the work.

I trust You, Lord. And just like Joshua and Caleb, I pray that <u>Your</u> name would be glorified. And that <u>everyone</u> who has seen T and I in this mess and to whom I have boldly said, "'The Lord is my helper, I shall not fear; what can man do to me?" (Hebrews 13:6)—My God has promised us healing and deliverance in this family. He <u>is</u> going to do this for us. We <u>will</u> be victorious,' will see the glory of the LORD when at last You bring us into the land which You have promised us, out of our captivity and into a land flowing with milk and honey."

Journal entry November 25, 2009:

"Numbers 14-15

Numbers 15:18 '<u>When</u> you come into the land to which I bring you...'

Numbers 15:2 'When you have come into the land you are to inhabit which I am giving you...'

Proverbs 20-21

Isaiah 40-41

Joel 2:25, Joel 2:21,32

Please, Father, I beg You with all my heart, let T call on Your name and be saved. Let him know the name of the LORD his God. Let him love the LORD his God with all his heart, all his soul, all his mind, and all his strength. Show him that I love him, Lord, that You love him even more. Bless him, Lord with Your Spirit. Let Your Spirit dwell in him and hover over him. I plead the blood of Jesus over T, myself, (our son, and our daughter) in this day. Please, Abba, I beg You, heal my family. Bring us back together once and for all. I know You did not bring me to this place just to leave me here and let us die in this wilderness. Help me to fight for my family with love, LORD, with Your love. No matter what darts the enemy tries to throw my way. Let me stop striving (Proverbs 20:3) and shower my husband with Your love, Lord. No matter what he says or does. Let me be Jesus to him. Let me be the Jesus he sees."

Journal entry November 30, 2009:

"Nehemiah 9

Psalm 78

The Israelites were so well taken care of; and yet they <u>kept</u> disobeying God. He was so patient with them; and then He firmly chastened them. And then had mercy on them again.

Isaiah 43. God's love and deliverance for <u>me.</u>

Philippians 4:8. Think on <u>good</u> things.

Psalm 78. God has given me wisdom into this passage. He has come through for my family and for <u>me</u> time and time again. He <u>always</u> takes care of us. He has never and will never let us down. I actually have joy and peace now, and things are just the same. But, like the Israelites, when something doesn't go my way, I lose faith and ask God to confirm His words to me over and over again, and then tell Him I don't believe Him, and act out. He is telling me just to <u>trust Him</u> and act in faith and <u>He will</u> take care of our family—our <u>whole</u> family.

Joshua 21:43-45 'So the LORD gave to Israel all the land of which He had sworn to give to their fathers, and they took possession of it and dwelt in it. The LORD gave them rest all around, according to all that He had sworn to their fathers. And not a man of all their enemies stood against them; the LORD delivered all their enemies into their hand. Not a word failed of any good thing which the LORD had spoken to the house of Israel. All came to pass.'"

Journal entry December 4, 2009:

"Ezekiel 34–37

I cried as I read of God's comfort and provision and love for me and for my family. He is my Good Shepherd and my Daddy, my Abba. My God. He loves me and these children, and T, so much. He is bringing us into our own land. A healed, married land. Lucy called yesterday and asked if she could read me Isaiah 62. She had no idea that God had given me this passage time and time again.

I love You so much, my Abba. You are incredible."

Journal entry December 8, 2009:

"Joel 2:21

Isaiah 43

2 Samuel 22

Father, please protect (my son and daughter) from insecurity, fear, anger, sadness, loneliness, abuse, violence. Keep their hearts and minds clean and pure and stayed on You. Show them just how special they are, Lord, and never, never let the disgusting curse of adultery be passed down to their families. Please, Lord, I pray right now that You would reverse the curse of anger and infidelity in my family and do not allow it to be passed down to my children. Father, I pray especially for (another family struggling with adultery). (The children) feel the world is against them. They feel insecure and frustrated because their daddy is gone and their world is crumbling. God, I beg You to bring their daddy back. I beg You to heal the wounds T and I have made in our children. Let both T and I exhibit love, joy, peace, patience, kindness, goodness, faithfulness, gentleness, and self-control. Let our <u>whole</u> family—T, Catherine, (our son and daughter)—love the LORD our God with all our hearts, all our souls, all our minds and all our strength. In Jesus' name I pray, amen."

Journal entry December 18, 2009:

"2 Chronicles 18. Praying against the lying prophets. Whatever the Lord says, I will speak. I Kings 13. I am fasting. I am very sad about my family. I miss my husband—not the way he was, because he was evil and cruel, but I miss him and am so disappointed in what our marriage has become. I have to keep trusting the Lord, who continues to tell me my marriage is healed. I am very tired. My kids are sad and miss their dad so much. I'm praying for their little spirits, because this is extremely damaging to them. I know the Lord can and will heal them, but that is my main area of sadness now, watching them grieve over their daddy being gone.

Psalm 74, 75, 76. God's protection for me from my enemies; my enemies' demise.

Job 37-38. God's awesome majesty.

Psalm 139-140. God's love for me; and my enemies' ill fate.

Jeremiah 33. God will heal our family. A marriage restored."

Journal entry December 23, 2009:

"Isaiah 64:4 'Men have not heard nor perceived by the ear, nor has the eye seen any God besides You, who acts for the one who waits for Him.'

I Chronicles 8

Help me not to be unfaithful, Lord. Help me to believe Your report and to trust in You and <u>glorify</u> Your name, no matter what. Please forgive me for doubting You."

Journal entry January 4, 2010:

"I Chronicles 8

I Kings 8:23. God keeps His covenant with us. He keeps <u>all</u> His promises.

Isaiah 43. Oh, how He loves <u>me</u>.

I am fasting my evening meal with J (dear friend) for 21 days (Daniel 10) to dedicate this year to my Abba.

Joel 2:25"

Journal entry January 8, 2010:

"Genesis 22:9

God wants me to sacrifice my life to Him so that I might be identified with Him—not for the mere end of my life being in death—but so that I might live <u>through</u> Him."

    Meanwhile, back at my new job, God introduced me to another lifeline friend who was also the Spanish teacher. We will call her "Susan." She was a strong Christian and was used by the Lord in a major way to encourage and speak life over both Sheila and me. She also fasted for breakthrough and occasionally God would have us participate in this warfare together against the enemy. She had never married, but was constantly in the Word and knew the deep power of prayer. She began to pray and speak God's truth over both Sheila and me. When others were telling us to divorce our husbands and get a fresh start, this prayer warrior teacher would say nothing of the sort. She continued to believe with us that God was still in the miracle-working business, and that He would deliver our families from Satan's grip.
    And then Sheila's miracle came. After months of praying and hoping for God's healing, and Sheila's continued talks with her husband, God began to turn this man's heart. God single-handedly broke up his extramarital affair and caused him to come home. Sheila had continued to pray for months for her husband to come home, and I had continually encouraged her not to proceed with the divorce. Then one day her attorney called and told her the divorce was dismissed. Neither she nor her husband had been communicating with their lawyers for weeks, and the case was simply dropped. I will never forget Sheila jumping around in the Pre-K room, gleefully explaining to me what had just happened. One by one, God put the pieces of their marriage and family back together after that. Sheila and her husband quickly moved back in together and began a new life of forgiveness and healing. Her husband gave his life to Christ. And, almost a year to the day I met her, their pastor re-married Sheila and her husband in front of their entire congregation. Many months later, these same people—Sheila and her husband and their two good friends who led

their small group—would be instrumental in our own family's healing. Our God is truly mind-blowing.

God allowed me to see His miraculous hand at work in the lives of so many others in and through this preschool/daycare. I was then and am now truly grateful for the opportunity God gave me there to love and to be loved on by so many new friends, several of whom I am still in contact with today. And while my own marriage was not yet restored, I was encouraged by what I had seen God do for my friend Sheila's marriage and family. It would be a long process of continual healing, but their victory continued to spur me on in faith and believing for my own family.

I hesitated to share this journal entry, simply because it felt so raw. After praying about it, my reason in sharing it here is to convey the fleshly struggle that obviously ensued during all of these years in hopes that my readers will identify, if need be, and also be able to resonate with a holy GOD who can do absolutely any miracle on their behalf.

CHAPTER 13

"You shall no longer be termed Forsaken, nor shall your land any more be termed Desolate; but you shall be called Hephzibah,* and your land Beulah; for the LORD delights in you, and your land shall be married. For as a young man marries a virgin, so shall your sons marry you; and as the bridegroom rejoices over the bride, so shall your God rejoice over you."

~ Isaiah 62:4-5

Out of the ash heap, God provided a deep heart-friend for me during these years, a friend who was in the original praying group of four moms with tots. Eerily, all four of the women in that group later discovered, one by one, that their husbands were also committing adultery. Two of us from the group decided to radically trust God for His healing. The other two divorced. This deep-heart friend, we will call her "Janice," had already seen evidence of her husband's infidelity when we were just getting to know each other. After I confronted my husband, we began to confide in each other. Her husband soon moved out as well, and we two were on our own with our children. But we were never alone. God proved Himself to us again and again. She and I remain bosom buddies to this day, because of the gut-wrenching trauma we experienced together. She too made a plan to trust the Lord in a no-holds-barred kind of way. God gave us each other to hold on to for dear life during these crisis years, and the ones to follow in the future. Our children became great friends. We constantly lifted each other up and bolstered one another. When one of us was about to throw in the towel, the other one would bring them back to God's truth and the remembrance of His promises. We fasted together. We prayed together on a regular basis, daily for a very long time. We watched God grow daisies in our piles of rubble. We watched Him work miracles out of thin air.

And there were other dear friends—some who had or were currently experiencing this kind of pain—and some who just came alongside our family for support in prayer and friendship and sometimes financial aid or to help with the children. God pulled friends out of the woodwork to surround our family by His ever-protecting, all-knowing hand. Some walked with us all the way. Others saw just a sliver of that season. But they were there, and only God could have brought them. I began to realize that not only were they ministering to me, but I was also ministering to them. Our family's message was a very real message of hope in a world gone hay-wire.

A close friend from our church who I met on our mission trip to South Africa many years before (we will call her "Wanda") was also going through a horrific attack on her marriage. We confided in each other and prayed together often. She was waiting on God for a very long time for His deliverance for her husband and for their marriage. Sadly, her marriage ended in divorce. What God began showing me through this time was that I was not an anomaly. This infidelity leading to divorce was an epidemic— even *and especially* among Christians—going on all over the country and all over our world. Now more than ever, Satan was threatening the very heart of God's army, the family. The enemy's aim was to disable our families completely, so as to render us incompetent as Christians to stand in the fight against him and win this war.

God never left us alone during what could have been a completely maddening season. He constantly brought joy in the midst of our sorrow. He brought His army around us to protect and to nurture our family, and to put us on a path toward healing. There is a group of four women I call my "Soul Sisters" to this day. We have gone through everything imaginable together. Births, deaths, infidelity, loss of career, adoption of children, missions at home and abroad, spousal pornography struggles, homicide of a family member by a family member, mental illness of family members, weddings, graduations, children's Biblical rite of passage ceremonies, sickness, financial struggles, rejoicing and sadness, beauty and pain, hearing God's voice and encouraging one another continually. For these women, I am eternally grateful. One of these precious sisters—we will call her "Julia"—began as a mentoring mom to the rest of us. In fact, we all met her at a Bible study called "Mother's Heart." She was one of two teachers at this study, discipling young moms to be godly wives and mothers. She was a missionary to the UK, Russia, and Ukraine for eighteen years. When she was stateside, she often held "retreats" in her home, where young wives and mothers could go to fellowship, rest, craft if they wanted, and just sit at the feet of Jesus and be loved on. She had then, and continues to have, such wisdom and grace and an incredible gift of hospitality, far beyond any I have ever seen or experienced. These women are words of wisdom and tears of joy, all of them. They truly know how to minister to those in need. To call them accountability partners is not in the least bit scratching the surface to describe their friendship to me and to my family over the years, although they definitely are that, each and every one of them. These friends are purer than gold—gifts of God to me that will last a lifetime.

I did learn during that period to be very discerning about who I let in to my world. There were many well-meaning Christians who simply were not able to hear God's voice of truth and His radical solution to this perplexing epidemic attacking our nation with a vengeance. I often began a conversation during that season in hopes of being a testimony to someone of God's vision for marriage, only to discover that the spirit of doubt resting on that person was too dangerous for me to interact with in this embryonic stage of God's rebirth for my family. I was a pupa emerging from my cocoon, and needed to shield myself from the enemy and his "messengers of light" at every turn. Satan masqueraded in many different ways, and I discovered during that time that he even often used Christians to do his dirty work. Thankfully, God began to teach me how to hear His own voice in a much more personal way, as He alerted me quickly and succinctly to these subtle attacks.

My extended family sometimes became a source of this kind of passive-aggressive attack by the enemy. Feeling the need for support, at the onset of my journey I often shared more than I should have with members of my family who wanted to help, but were not really equipped to do so. I learned quickly that this radical path was not for the faint of heart. There were a few family members that I could share with, though, and who committed to walking with me in prayer and believing for my marriage and family. God was fine-tuning my heart and quickening my spirit to hear His voice much more immediately. I learned to know when God's hand was up, meaning, **"No, don't speak"** in stark contrast to His peace in my heart, giving me the nod to go ahead. God really did not waste a moment during all of those seemingly dark days of our lives. I sometimes did, but He never wasted any of the time. His loving arms were constantly around me and around my children, His voice behind us saying, "This is the way. Walk in it" (Isaiah 30:21).

Hephzibah (Hebrew) is translated "My delight is in her."

CHAPTER 14

"I have set watchmen on your walls, O Jerusalem; they shall never hold their peace day or night."

~ Isaiah 62:6

God confirmed Himself to me and to my children over and over again in those four years. He constantly took me to Joel 2:25-26. I cannot count the number of times I would sit in my chair at His feet and open His book directly to the page with those verses on it. And there were other scriptures He just repeated to me time and time again. Isaiah 60-62 was like the banner for my family. He spoke to me everywhere I went. God was in everything. On the radio, in dear friends' voices, in my pastor's voice, in my children's voices. He spoke to them too, and they were listening. We all were.

One night after the children were asleep, I opened the bedroom door to check on them. They were both sleeping in the bunkbeds in my son's room. My heart was breaking as I cried out to God for their lives, "Please show me something, God. Please tell me they are gonna be ok." Right then, the eyes of my heart were opened to see two extremely tall angels standing floor to ceiling—one at the head and one at the foot of those bunkbeds. They were glowing like candlelight and standing completely still. They were peaceful, but they were definitely warriors. They were looking straight ahead at my children. They were on guard for their lives. I can still remember that vision. What a gift from the Lord. I did not need to question their safekeeping. They were completely in His grip. It was probably about that time that I began praying the Aaronic blessing over my children. It is found in Numbers 6:23 and proclaims, "The LORD bless you and keep you; the LORD make His face shine upon you, and be gracious to you; the LORD lift up His countenance upon you, and give you peace." Years later I would begin to doubt the precious vision of the angels the Lord had given me. But even then, in His great mercy, God continued to confirm what He had already shown me.

There was much back and forth for my husband and I over the next three years. He came home several times, and we tried to make things work. But each time he left, I was disappointed and disgruntled. I struggled to hang on to the victorious vision the Lord had given me for this family. Each time we failed at patching things up, our children were also dragged through the mud, and no doubt struggled with feelings of hopelessness. I know our son struggled with anger during those years, and me right along with him. I was often on my knees, fasting and praying and asking the Lord over and over to help me to forgive.

God constantly showered His love on the kids and me. One night in January of 2010, I had a dream. Two friends, at least one from my work, were blessing me with gifts. When I awoke, the devotional I read was about Simone the Cyrene bearing Jesus' cross. It talked about my obedience costing others, but that this was what God had for them and that I was not to try and relieve them of this cost. I took it to mean generosity, and that I was not to turn it away. The very next day, my dear friend Sheila from work offered me her mother's car, a Durango that was a few years old, but still in good condition. She said I could pay her whatever I could afford on a monthly basis. I had given my sister's car back by this time and had taken over payments on a different family member's car by now, but it was too expensive for me to afford on my daycare salary. This Durango was a true need. The day after that, another friend of mine called and asked me what she could bring me from the grocery store. One day, my friend Janice told me she was treating me to a Christian concert that would take place the following month. Then she showed up at my job with a bag of clothes and makeup for me. My Soul Sister Julia took me to lunch one day, and invited me to an overnight retreat at her lake house the following month. My aunt and uncle in Austin invited the kids and I to come down and relax at their house in the woods with them. And my Soul Sister Lucy invited me to an overnight at her home. God was bountifully pouring out his abundant blessings over the children and me. All for His glory.

Journal entry January 11, 2010:

"Joel 2:21-25

The Lord <u>will</u> restore to us the years the locusts have eaten.

Luke 23:26. *My Uttmost for His Highest*, Oswald Chambers. My obedience costs others more than me. Do not quench the Holy Spirit by pridefully refusing to accept what He has laid on their hearts to give."

One of the things God began to reveal to me during those dark days was my propensity to anger, even rage. Truthfully, this had been going on since I was a young child. I tried to mask it in all sorts of ways; but when push came to shove, the mask came off and there was no hiding my inability to control my temper. As I read back through my journals, even to write this book, I am weeping at the thought of how I hurt my children's hearts in those days. They were completely helpless to defend themselves against my rage, once the monster was unleashed. No matter how many times I apologized and asked their forgiveness, I could not retract the wounds I made. Eventually God would heal even these deep wounds, though, for all of us.

In February of 2010, the children and I joined an established, Bible-teaching church right in our community in obedience to a word I heard from the Lord. We had been visiting this church (our previous home church was forty-five minutes away) off and on occasionally for several years. There had been some signs from God over the last several months that He was changing our church home. Nevertheless, the absence of the spiritual family we knew and loved would leave a great hole in our hearts for a very long time to come. One Sunday we were in attendance at this new church, when I knew the Lord was saying **"Today is the day."** Right after I heard the Lord's prompting in my heart, the pastor invited anyone who would like to be a member of their church to do so after the service. I knew that day it was the time for us to take the plunge. The children and I went immediately after the service and spoke with the precious man in the welcoming department, who is a pillar of the church, and had our pictures made.

That same day, I had also visited, and God said *"join,"* a Bible fellowship group in the morning before the big service. I will have to say I was really resisting doing ALL of this. I did not love change (probably because my life had been one never-ending change up to that point!) and I definitely did not want to bring any new people into our mix at that time. But God said, *"Go,"* so I obeyed. It would not be long before the Lord asked me to voice my prayer request for our marriage to be restored before this new group, and me sitting right on the front row. Not coincidentally, I am sure, I was "placed" in the very group with most of the families from our children's school who were members of this church. I got the feeling, like it or not, God was going to use me and use our story in a major way here. Ok God, it's YOUR SHOW. Have Thine own way, LORD! Ironically, about two weeks after the children and I joined this new church, the esteemed pastor who had shepherded that flock for eleven years obeyed the Lord's call to leave, and go back to the church he had come from as associate pastor. My heart was broken. What was the Lord doing? I remember sobbing as the children and I arrived home that Sunday afternoon. But I had to trust God. He had instructed us to join this fellowship of believers. He undoubtedly knew exactly what He was doing.

One day a few weeks later, I was at church on Sunday and I felt the Holy Spirit prompting me to join a specific home group. This was my second or third nudge from the Lord on this subject. I asked the Lord to show me the woman (we will call her "Darci") who had constantly sought us out at this point, if He really wanted me to do this thing. She found me right after the service was over. Sitting in church, I had seen a vision in my mind's eye of the home group praying and being instrumental to bring my husband home. So, when Darci showed up at the end of the service that day, it was not a surprise. I obeyed the Lord, and we decided to start meeting with these few families once a week. One Sunday, two weeks after we joined the group, I shared with them my prayer request for our marriage to be healed. Interestingly, the study we were doing *(The Prodigal God*[16]*)* was on the Prodigal Son, a story the Lord had repeatedly given me in His Word for my husband. Through tears that evening, I explained that my husband was living the life of the prodigal son, but that God had promised me a marriage restored. The support I felt that night was great. There were some barriers I had sensed the week before which were no longer there. I felt a connection with at least three of the women. When my children and I left that night, I thanked God for His faithfulness and for helping me to be obedient to His call on my life, even when I felt afraid.

    God poured into me in those days. They were very purposeful. Every day, I sat at His feet and He filled me up. The Lord took that precious time to begin really teaching me how much He loved me and who I truly am in Christ. He opened my heart to His love. He showed me how closed-up my heart had been all of my life due to fear and anger. He took His time with me. God knew more than anyone all of the damage that had been done to my heart, and what it would truly take to unravel this mess. We were in a quandary, no doubt. But there was no accident here. God knew exactly what He was doing, and He was right on time. He also knew exactly what it would take to actually get me to listen to Him—to finally really listen. All of my life I had heard about God's love for me and known, at least with my mind, that He was a loving God. I knew, because I was supposed to know, that He loved me. Because God loves everybody, right? But I never truly knew or felt God's love for me all of those years. Satan had really done a number on my soul, telling me lies I had been agreeing with for oh-so-many years. I didn't even know I was agreeing with the lie. It was just part of my makeup, like breathing. I knew what I truly thought about myself, deep down inside. I didn't talk about it often and mostly tried to hide it. But if you asked me, I knew it with certainty. I just didn't know where those thoughts originated. I didn't truly understand that the enemy of my soul had a plan to destroy me from day one. As I sat with my Heavenly Father though, day after day, and night after night, His truth over me became the banner by which I began to be known. My doubt and fear were being replaced by hope and faith. My anger was being replaced by love. Violence was being replaced by self-control. Bitterness was being replaced by forgiveness. Depression was being replaced by joy. Anxiety was being replaced by peace. Insecurity was being replaced by strength in Christ. Guilt was being replaced by grace. God was replacing the lie with His truth.

    And I couldn't keep it to myself. Because of *the veil being lifted from my spirit*, I wanted to shout God's glory to the world. I looked for opportunities to share this fascinating thing that God was doing in my life. And He gave them again and again.

On March 30, 2010 God placed a man right in my husband's path. The man was my friend Sheila's husband (we will call him "Paul"), whom God had recently returned home to live with his family. The week prior I had fasted for three days, during which time the Lord repeatedly told me to pray for someone to be placed in my husband's path (and also my friend Janice's husband's—Janice and I were praying this together). The following Tuesday, my husband had to go to the automobile dealership where Paul worked, as part of a routine sales call. My husband had started a new digital marketing business, and this dealership was his first customer. He walked into Paul's office. Immediately upon recognizing him he said, "Don't I know you?" Paul said, "Yes, I'm (Sheila's) husband. Our wives work together. How're you doing?" To which my husband replied, "Not good." Clearly, they both knew what he meant by that statement. Paul remarked that my husband had a beautiful daughter. My husband thanked him and asked how he was doing. Paul then proceeded to glorify the Lord with his testimony of how God was healing his marriage and family. He told my husband that he was going to church and that they were doing well. Paul came home and told his wife the story that evening, and she gushingly relayed what details she knew to me the very next day. All I could do was to glorify God for this glimpse of heaven. He knew right where we were at ALL times, and He was not going to let us go.

Meanwhile, my husband was living with the adulteress and her children. At least twice in a few months' time span, upon arriving at their house, his phone pocket-dialed me so that I could hear their entire conversation. As gut wrenching as this all was, I was still grateful to the Lord for showing me truth. God knew I was getting lulled to sleep a little too. My husband and I had engaged in some decent conversations recently, where we were getting along and things seemed to be going well between us. Just two days before this last telling intermission, God had spoken to me in a dream instructing me to fast yet again. I obeyed. He was working miracles I could not see through this powerful mechanism of fasting and prayer. I loved my Lord and was devoted to Him. Even though it was often painful, I would not willfully disobey Him at this point in my life.

No matter what, I knew beyond the shadow of a doubt that He alone had my back.

All around me there were signs of God's goodness and His faithfulness to me and to my family. For one thing, we never had to leave our beloved home during this entire journey. The children and I were privileged to stay right there in the comfort of our own home and let God lavish His goodness upon us daily, even though things looked different than we would have liked for them to. And He was constantly speaking to us. He kept giving me Joel 2:25-26, telling me He WOULD restore the years the locusts had eaten; and then He began showing me locusts and their wings! The Holy Spirit just began diverting my attention to all of the locust wings in our backyard one day. Then a few days later, one of my students at the preschool actually brought me one! My heart leaped for joy as this child handed me the wing from the ground.

One of the most precious blessings to me that year was that our daughter gave her heart to Jesus. The children and I were on our way home from church one Sunday morning when she began asking questions about heaven. I explained that she would be in God's family and would go to heaven when she died if she asked Jesus to come into her heart and to be her Savior. I explained that we all had sin in our lives, but that Jesus came to the earth from heaven to be our sacrifice for sin because He loved us just that much. I told of His death on a cross, and how He did not stay in the ground when He was buried, but rose from the dead on the third day after He died and was in heaven now preparing a place for His children to come home to. She said right then that she wanted to be a part of God's family. Not wanting her to rush her decision, I tried to prolong the conversation, until at least we were out of the car. She was adamant, though, insisting that she understood and that she most definitely wanted Jesus to be living in her heart! Our son, sitting with her in the backseat, was all too eager to lead her to Jesus that afternoon. He asked her to bow her head with him as he prayed a simple prayer and had her repeat the words after him. He couldn't wait to lead his sister to Jesus. I will never forget that day. What a great reminder that in the midst of all our trial and sorrows, God had not forgotten about us. Even my children were hearing the voice of the Holy Spirit with alacrity.

CHAPTER 15

"'Sing, O daughter of Zion! Shout, O Israel! Be glad and rejoice with all your heart, O daughter of Jerusalem! The LORD has taken away your judgements, He has cast out your enemy. The King of Israel, the LORD, is in your midst; You shall see disaster no more. In that day it shall be said to Jerusalem: "Do not fear; Zion, let not your hands be weak, the LORD your God in your midst, the Mighty One, will save; He will rejoice over you with gladness, He will quiet you with His love, He will rejoice over you with singing.

I will gather those who sorrow over the appointed assembly, who are among you, to whom its reproach is a burden. Behold, at that time I will deal with all who afflict you; I will save the lame, and gather those who were driven out; I will appoint them for praise and fame in every land where they were put to shame. At that time I will bring you back, even at the time I gather you; for I will give you fame and praise among all the peoples of the earth, when I return your captives before your eyes,' says the LORD."

~ Zephaniah 3:14-20

At the end of April of 2010, a year and four months after I started my job at the preschool, God told me it was time to come home from work. He had been speaking about this to me for a few weeks by this time, and had opened up several part-time and seasonal opportunities that would allow me to be home with my children. I was overjoyed. When I walked into the office that afternoon to give my notice to the owner, I knew she understood that this had been more than a job to me. I wept as I told her I was leaving—she said she knew it was coming. She told me I was welcome back anytime I needed a job.

Journal entry April 28th, 2010:

"I have quit my job at (the daycare). It was a wonderful gift from the LORD which I will always cherish. My last day is May 21st, the day after (our son's) last day of school. I am going to work markets five times a year. The Lord totally gave me a name and I was hired over the phone immediately to sell their contemporary jeans, and run a sample sale out of my home which C (friend) will be turning over to me. 'Just so happens' that she just had her last sale after ten years and is willing to give me all her contacts/lines and show me the ropes. I'm also going to be a baby clothes rep and do direct sales for 'boutiquey' baby clothes at home parties. I may also direct-sell men's custom shirts. I have a meeting with C today. We'll see what the Lord says! All of this will afford me the flexibility to be home with my kiddos full time!!!"

Journal entry April 29th, 2010:

"Meeting went well!

I went to Sheila and Paul's Bible study last night. Kind of surreal to be sitting there with Paul, who is now praying for my husband. Very strange and wonderful indeed. Oddly enough, the Lord had given (Paul's friend), Paul and me all the same verse over the past two days (Paul said he was reading there that morning. WOW!) It is Romans 8:18."

Paul's friend had also heard God tell him to pray for the Lord to make His face shine on our desolate sanctuary—not because we deserved it, but because of His great mercies and for His own sake—and to forgive us, the people who are called by His name (Daniel 9:17-19). This become one of the things I asked God for regularly. The verse, a prayer from Daniel to God, reads, "Now therefore, our God, hear the prayer of Your servant, and his supplications, and for the Lord's sake cause Your face to shine on Your sanctuary, which is desolate. O my God, incline Your ear and hear; open Your eyes and see our desolations, and the city which is called by Your name; for we do not present our supplications before You because of our righteous deeds, but because of Your great mercies. O Lord, hear! O Lord, forgive! O Lord, listen and act! Do not delay for Your own sake, my God, for Your city and Your people are called by Your name." Not long after that, this special group of friends each took a day one week and fasted for breakthrough for me and for my family. I felt so completely loved on and cherished by the Father, and knew that He was up to something *mighty*.

> Journal entry May 13, 2010:
>
> "2 Chronicles 31
>
> The people had all they needed because they joyfully and faithfully gave their tithes and burnt offerings to the LORD.
>
> I love You, Lord! Thank You for constantly taking care of my little family (insert smiley face!).
>
> We worship You!!!"

Journal entry May 14, 2010:

"Joshua 21:43-45

'So the LORD gave to Israel all the land of which He had sworn to give to their fathers, and they took possession of it and dwelt in it. The LORD gave them rest all around, according to all that He had sworn to their fathers. And not a man of all their enemies stood against them; the LORD delivered all their enemies into their hand. Not a word failed of any good thing which the LORD had spoken to the house of Israel. *All came to pass*' (italics mine)."

I was believing God for some pretty big miracles. There was no turning back, unless I was going to shuck everything I knew up to this point and tune in to my pain, fear, and pride. Either I had been believing a lie, imagining every single time the Lord spoke His specific words over my life, in His Word, through my dreams and visions, and through all of the other means He had chosen so far to get my attention—or it was all truth. The God of the universe really did still speak to His children in miraculous and uncanny (as well as sometimes ordinary) ways—or He didn't, and I was making it all up. There was only one way to find out. I had to trust Him. I was ALL IN.

Journal entry May 15, 2010:

"I Samuel 15:22-24

I Samuel 16

Samuel doubted God; and God surprised Him. God always comes through in His own way, in His own time, so we can never say it was our plan or by our might or by our power. Thank You so much, LORD, for bringing me home from work and for instilling in my children the power of prayer. Yesterday, we were with (my stepdad and stepmom) and they were asking me about what I was doing, now that I would be staying home. After I explained, (our son) piped up and said, 'Mom, tell them what we prayed!'—which was, of course, the most important part of the story!

Ecclesiastes 13-14"

Journal entry May 17, 2010:

"Exodus 10-13

God hardened Pharaoh's heart to show His glory. He single-handedly saved His people, Israel, from the Egyptians. His same pillar of cloud was thick darkness to the Egyptians, but a light to His own people.

Joshua 11:20

The LORD hardened the hearts of those who came against Israel in battle—that He might utterly destroy them—for His glory.

Joshua 11:23 'So Joshua took the whole land according to all that the LORD had said to Moses; and Joshua gave it as an inheritance to Israel according to their divisions by their tribes. Then the land rested from war.'

Exodus 14:14 'The LORD will fight for you, and you shall hold your peace.'

Exodus 14:13 'Do not be afraid. Stand still, and see the salvation of the LORD, which He will accomplish for you today.'"

Journal entry May 20, 2010:

"Isaiah 60, 61, 62

My precious children. The LORD will heal their broken hearts (Isaiah 60:22).

Healing for my heart and for our entire family (Isaiah 62:11).

I Kings 8:23 'There is no god in heaven above or on earth below like You, who keep Your covenant and mercy with Your servants who walk before You with all their hearts.'"

Journal entry May 31, 2010:

"Romans 16:20 'And the God of peace will crush Satan under your feet shortly. The grace of our Lord Jesus Christ be with you. Amen.'

I Corinthians 1:27 'But God has chosen the foolish things of the world to put to shame the wise, and God has chosen the weak things of the world to put to shame the things which are mighty.'

I Corinthians 2:9 '"Eye has not seen, nor ear heard, nor have entered into the heart of man the things which God has prepared for those who love Him"' (also Isaiah 64:4).

I Corinthians 1:31 'He who glories, let him glory in the LORD.'

I Corinthians 3:6-8 'I planted, Apollos watered (Paul speaking here), but God gave the increase. So then neither he who plants is anything, nor he who waters, but GOD who gives the increase. Now he who plants and he who waters are one, and each one will receive his own reward according to his own labor.'

Joel 2:25 'So I will restore to you the years that the swarming locust has eaten, the crawling locust, the consuming locust, and the chewing locust, my great army which I sent among you. You shall eat in plenty and be satisfied, and praise the name of the LORD your God.'

Psalm 10:16-18

Nehemiah 8:10

Jonah 2

Nehemiah 9

Ezra 8

The Lord is telling me to fast today. I will gladly obey Him because I love Him so very much."

Journal entry June 14, 2010:

"Pray for wisdom. He gave me the story of Solomon two times this morning. I read it to the kids. (Our son) picked out the little Bible story book to read, and I opened <u>right</u> up to the story in I Kings 3 when I had my time alone w/

God. Solomon could have prayed for riches and/or power, but he prayed for wisdom. God gave him all three.

Pray for peace. John 14:27.

Pray for freedom from insecurity & freedom from the fear of abandonment.

Pray for freedom from fear, anxiety and anger.

Psalm 107. God will deliver me from destruction, help (me) the afflicted & bring judgment on my enemies.

God loves _me_ so very much."

Journal entry June 15, 2010:

"Ecclesiastes 9:9-12

I am to pray for T to live joyfully with the wife whom he loves all the days of his vain life which the LORD has given him."

Journal entry June 16, 2010:

"2 Samuel 3:16

I am to pray that T will be weeping behind me.

Deuteronomy 28:7

I am to pray that the LORD will cause my enemies who rise against me to be defeated before my face; they shall come out against me one way & flee before me seven ways.

Psalm 127. Pray to treat my children as a heritage from the LORD & a reward.

Psalm 128. Pray for T to fear the Lord & to walk in His ways & for me to be a fruitful vine in the very heart of our house, & our children like olive plants all around our table."

Journal entry June 25, 2010:

"John 12:24 'Most assuredly, I say to you, unless a grain of wheat falls into the ground and dies, it remains alone; but if it dies, it produces much grain.'

Please, Lord, let T and I and (our son and daughter) die to ourselves and live in You, that we may be raised in the newness of Your life.

Let T fear You, Lord, and let me be like a fruitful vine in the middle of our home. Let our children be like olive plants all around the table."

Journal entry June 29, 2010:

"I am praying for T to be released from the bondage of adultery and lust. I am praying for T and (the adulteress) to repent and give their lives to Christ.

Hosea 14:4-9. I prayed this prayer of wisdom and truth and righteousness over our family and over T.

Joel 2:25-26"

Journal entry July 3, 2010:

"Isaiah 59-60

Isaiah 59:20. My children will be saved from the sin of adultery because of my faithfulness.

Salvation, righteousness and justice for my family

Isaiah 60:22 "'A little one shall become a thousand, and a small one a strong nation. I the LORD, will hasten it in its time.'"

Satan may <u>not</u> have my children. They are the Lord's.

Salvation for my marriage

Isaiah 61-62

The sons of the foreigner shall not drink my new wine for which I have labored.

'But those who have gathered it shall eat it (the wheat?) and praise the LORD, those who have brought it together shall drink it in my holy courts.' Isaiah 62:8-9

Matthew 9:16-17

John 12:24

Wow! The Lord has given me this passage (Isaiah 60-62) <u>many</u> times, and again today to remind me of His promise to me, His covenant with me. The Lord just reminded me last night through *Experiencing God*[17] that if (when) He speaks and makes a promise to me, He <u>will</u> keep it, no matter how long it takes to manifest."

Unveiled

God was showing me (Micah 4 & 5) that this deliverance was definitely not going to be easy. In fact, He compared it to a birthing process. He told me that we would be delivered through pangs of labor in the very place where our destruction began. In other words, He was not going to move us to a far-away country to some mountaintop where we could get away from everyone we had been in community with all of this time. No, our healing would take place here, where people we saw and knew and loved and interacted with daily were praying for us and had witnessed these cataclysmic events that threatened to destroy our family beyond recognition. And yet HE would get ALL of the glory.

He was equally showing me how much He loved *me*, and that I needed to continue to pray and to trust Him to change me as a wife and mother. He was not responsible for my circumstances. But He had allowed my pain and our family's tragic events to bring us strength in Him, grow us up in Him and draw us all nearer to His heart. I was ever praying for God to remove my temper tantrums and to allow me to love my husband and my children with a true Christ-like love. I was asking Him to help me to "be Jesus" to my family in humility, peace, gentleness, kindness, truth and self-sacrifice—to love them just like He did. As our young son grew older, I was beginning to realize his strong-willed personality, which I now understand is also part of his incredible gift of God-given leadership. (I would learn later that God blessed me with two strong-willed children. Our daughter is also a *force*, spiritually speaking.) I prayed that God would give me a loving, patient heart to replace my often anxious, angry, fearful, perfection-seeking heart. I realized then that my attitude was contributing to my children's sadness, insecurity, anger and behavior problems. God began showing me that I could instead have a spiritual response—not always a fleshly response—to their behavior, and that kind, soft but firm words of wisdom *work*. What a concept, right?! I was truly grateful to the Lord again for loving me (and my children!) enough to patiently show me how to love them.

He also continued to give me Hebrews 11:1, "Now faith is the substance of things hoped for, the evidence of things not seen." Well, good. Because I clearly wasn't seeing any of this yet.

He continued reminding me that I didn't have to be afraid and that I didn't need to DO anything but pray and trust Him, and that He, the

Lord, would fight for me. I was to hold my peace, be still and let Him do the heavy lifting (Exodus 14:13-14). Good again, because I was so tired. The Holy Spirit also directed me several times to Lamentations 2:19 which says, "Pour out your heart like water before the face of the Lord. Lift your hands toward Him for the life of your young children." Clearly the Lord knew just how much my children were hurting. My job was to pray for them constantly, and to trust Him with their very lives.

During this time, a much-loved associate pastor from our new church—we will call him "Pastor Raymond"—was leading a smaller portion of the body on Sunday mornings in a separate, less formal venue from the main sanctuary, still on the church campus. The children and I often attended this service and soon became regulars there. Eventually I came to know Raymond (it would have been hard to be under his teaching and not get to know him; he is just that kind of guy), and one Sunday, he learned a little about our story. Right away, he placed me with an anointed woman who would soon become one of the best mentors I have ever known and one of my very closest friends. We will call her "Linda." She would walk with me in this journey and pray over our family from that day forward, always a listening ear and a heart full of wisdom. And what a prayer warrior!!! Intercessory prayer is truly one of her greatest spiritual gifts, among many others. For decades, she was one of the backbone prayer warriors of this church, being faithful to meet with a few other women at the church every Wednesday to pray over the specific needs of the body and leadership. God has given her countless "assignments" over the years, and she has accepted each one with the utmost sincerity and care. She never enters into prayer lightly. She knows when she speaks to God, she is speaking directly to the Author and Creator of the universe, and that He knows her by name. We would form a friendship that day that would last a lifetime. She soon began calling herself my "Texas Mama." And I agreed.

One of the verses the Lord regularly gave me during that time was Esther 2:17. It reads, "The king loved Esther more than all the *other* women, and she obtained grace and favor in his sight more than all the virgins, so he set the royal crown upon her head and made her queen instead of Vashti." God was telling me then that His hand was upon me, He had favor on me. His love for me was so great. I was beautiful in His sight. He was honoring me among women. I stuck out in a crowd to Him. My life mattered and I was special to my Heavenly Father. I was a pearl of great price—my worth was far above rubies. He had formed me and made me very carefully, and He was proud of His work. It was good.

Also, the Lord was showing me here that He was clearly taking His time in preparing me to be His servant, His queen, the bride of Christ, just as Esther and the other virgins (how awesome that He referred to me this way, also signifying my redemption in Christ!) spent an entire year in beauty preparation before they met with King Ahasuerus (Esther 2:12-13). God wanted me to be a godly and beautiful wife to my husband, and godly mama to our son and daughter—patient, humble, kind, good, submissive to my husband and to God, respectful, peaceful, wise and a good steward of all He had given us. And if it took years for me to learn this stuff, so be it.

Funny—as the years went on, I forgot what I knew from the Lord that very first time He gave me the passage in Esther. In fact, I would come to believe that God was giving me this passage to describe how my *husband's* love for me would again be someday. Even if that were true, it would not be enough. Another *person's* love is never good enough to fill us completely or to give us what we need, no matter who they are or how much they love. People will *always* fail us. They will always let us down in their humanity at some point or another. That's just the way it is. It happened in the fall of Adam and Eve. God created a perfect world, but man sinned—and we are left with death unless we trust in Christ for salvation from those sins. But even when we do trust Christ as our Savior, we are still only human. One human can never satisfy another human completely.

That's where God comes in. God and *only God*. It wasn't until very recently that I realized this very profound *Esther* word from the Lord again. He spoke these words to me that night, just as I was going to bed, and right then I realized that every time He took me to that passage over the last few years, He was telling me of <u>His</u> love for <u>me</u>. He loves me beyond words. No one can ever snatch me out of His hand. It is an incredible, amazing, heart-pounding, gut-wrenching, Holy-Spirit-fire, never-to-be-quenched, you-just-can't stop-it kind of never-ending love. He knows all my thoughts and feelings and sin and remorse and guilt and shame and shortcomings and pitfalls and that I'm gonna do it again. And yet, He chooses to love me. This is just the way He loves His children. He runs hard after us. His love is unfathomable to me.

In September of that year, as I continued to pray for the Lord to cause His face to shine on our desolate sanctuary, He showed me a very important truth in His Word. It is located in the book of Daniel, in the same passage with this prayer. At this time in history, Daniel was fasting before God regarding the seventy-years' desolations of Jerusalem prophesied by the prophet Jeremiah. Daniel was praying fervently, following a very intense end-times vision from God. During this time, the angel Gabriel, who was present in this heavenly vision, came to speak with Daniel. He said, "O Daniel, I have now come forth to give you skill to understand. At the beginning of your supplications the command went out, and I have come to tell *you*, for you *are* greatly beloved; therefore consider the matter, and understand the vision…" (Daniel 8:1-9:27). God was showing me that my fasting was seen as a humble act before the Lord and was not taken lightly. God was helping me to understand that He begins to act, also sending angels to minister and work on our behalf, immediately the moment we take up that intense spiritual posturing of fasting and prayer. He does not take our pain or devotion with a grain of salt. We matter completely to Him. Psalm 10:17-18 also reveals this truth. The author pens, "LORD, You have heard the desire of the humble; You will prepare their heart; You will cause Your ear to hear, to do justice to the fatherless and the oppressed, that the man of the earth may oppress no more." I was beginning to get the picture.

CHAPTER 16

"Say to the daughter of Zion, 'Surely your salvation is coming; behold, His reward is with Him.' And they shall call them The Holy People; the Redeemed of the LORD; and you shall be called Sought Out, A City Not Forsaken."

~ Isaiah 62:11-12

January 15, 2011, I awoke in the night from a dream. I had been praying and had fallen asleep; It was the second day of a three-day fast. In my dream I heard the words, ***"Do not give up. Do not give up."***

God was doing big things in my family, and also opening my eyes to many other spiritual dragons all around us. Not only was our new church not really helping to address our situation, but I had become increasingly aware that it was harboring many other failed marriages and marriages in crisis as well. And the Christians seemed clueless—as a church, as a community, as a nation, about the growing epidemic of adultery. No one was really addressing this monster attacking thousands upon thousands of Christian marriages all over the world. It seemed many American Christians were just playing church. Checking the box, but not truly honoring God with their lives.

One of the highlights of that year was our son's baptism. He was very excited and had been talking about it for months, even years by that time. We asked Pastor Raymond to baptize him, as he was special to our family and influential in our healing. My husband was present and part of our celebration, along with our extended family. I think we all felt a glimmer of hope on that special day, like a lighthouse in the storm all around us.

On May 31, 2011, my husband moved back home with our family again. We had a rocky time—some big highs and some even bigger lows. God knew we weren't really ready yet, and within two and a half months, my husband was gone again. The adultery monster had surfaced one more time. God showed me in scripture that my husband was being unfaithful, then that truth was confirmed when I confronted him. He moved into his own apartment immediately. But God told me to be of good courage, and that HE WOULD heal our marriage once and for all. I just needed to trust Him, and to wait on Him.

Waiting on the Lord is one of the easiest, yet hardest things to do. If our brains will at once calm down and our spirits will trust in the truth of our Creator, we can rest in Him and cast all of our cares on Him. But when the enemy interferes with fearful thoughts, followed by prideful ones, we are doomed if we follow his lead. We will never succeed in that way. We will have no peace, but only anxiety and fear if we listen to the lies of the enemy. One of the most difficult things to do is to hear God telling us a hard truth about our lives, coupled with the knowledge that He wants us to *stay* in that situation and *not move*. To *believe God about the truth He is telling us*, truth involving an earthly circumstance that would produce fear to the average bear, and then to trust Him in the storm, instead of *running*—this goes against everything we know in our frail humanity.

But I can tell you with absolute certainty that following God here in this tough place, really resting in His bosom and *trusting Him implicitly* and *being still* when He commands, brings a supernatural peace and a strength beyond all human understanding. Perception is <u>not</u> reality. Satan *is* a liar and an accuser and will bring things before us that we fear, and will try and make us think they are real. Don't fall for it. Stand still and see the salvation of the Lord. Go when He says, **"Go."** Stand still when He says, **"Stand."** Listen to His voice and seek wisdom and discernment. We who are born again in Christ have a spiritual inheritance! We must pursue it with the Lord. The enemy will continue to attack us in the areas he knows have been promised to us. The Israelites fought 39 battles after they received their promise of the land of their inheritance from the Lord (Joshua 1-21, Joshua 21:43-45). We *must continue* to war in the heavenly places. We must trust GOD for our inheritance.

God took this time to show me other ways that I could come up higher. Guarding my tongue, controlling my temper, praying for God to take my defensive attitude, being vulnerable to my husband and openly showing him respect were just a few. These changes were not easy to make or even to *pray* about making in my current state. Everything in my flesh cried out to defend myself and run and hurl insults at my husband every chance I got. But I knew that was not what Christ was calling me to. And since I had decided I was *all in*, I had better give it my best shot and obey all of what God was telling me to do, not just the easier parts. This definitely required God humbling me some more, because in my own strength—and, let's face it, *pride*—I was ill-equipped. These new changes were going to require supernatural strength and giving *my will* over to God.

On July 27, 2011, I awoke from another God-given dream. My husband and the children and I were on vacation. We were in a dark, uninviting camp-like room with bunkbeds. The bedding was the same as the real-life bedding my husband had bought for his new apartment when he left our family. In the dream, we had been on this excursion together for many days, and it had been a pretty miserable time. My husband was acting distant and cold and purposefully withdrawing from me. He was intentionally withholding love and intimacy from me. It was not a good scene. Then, the scene changed. We were with another couple, watching a foot race. The other man was white with blondish hair. He had a glass of red wine with him. We were all sitting on bleachers—the man, his wife, my husband and me. I don't really remember the wife, I just know that she was there. All of a sudden, *my* husband began acting free and joyful and giddy. He picked up the other man's glass and took a sip with liberty. Knowing that I was doubting this extreme change in his demeanor, he said to me, "I don't know what happened before, but it was like I was walking in darkness. All I know now is that the chains are off; and I've been set free. *Like a veil has been lifted*." Immediately, I believed him. I knew he was telling the truth. The next scene was back at the camp where we had been vacationing. We were in the room with the bunkbeds, but this time, the light was on. There was a huge hole in the wall, and I knew that my family and my husband's family were present. But the only people I remember for certain were my husband, his father, and me. Apparently, his family thought I made the huge hole. They were blaming me. Then a man stood up and said to my husband's father, "It's not Catherine's fault." I believe the man speaking was my husband.

The next morning, the Lord took me to Esther 2, then Mark 10. Finally, He took me to Isaiah 62—a healed portrait of a beautiful marriage. Verses 8-9 say, "And the sons of the foreigner shall not drink your new wine, for which you have labored. But those who have gathered it shall eat it, and praise the LORD; Those who have brought it together shall drink it in My holy courts."

Two days later, our daughter had a dream. She said Jesus came down to earth and she hugged him—she and her brother hugged Him. Then Jesus was going to take them back to heaven with Him. She said when she woke up, she thought the whole family was in heaven. I was so grateful to hear our daughter tell of Jesus' love for her. God was so sweetly nurturing His precious babes in this giant storm.

God began showing me during this time just how much insecurity I had struggled with over the years, and that *insecurity is actually a sin*.[18] We are unable to be in God's will if we are insecure. Insecurity causes us to want to control people, and that is against God. I began asking the Lord to please deliver me from this insecurity once and for all, in Jesus' mighty name.

God also showed me then that He was working out longsuffering in me. My dear friend Wanda pointed this out one night as we confided in each other. God was freeing me from insecurity and giving me the spirit of longsuffering, the spirit of joy, and of a broken and contrite heart.

In November of 2011, I had a dream. I was walking into my house, but it was not exactly the same house. It was a pleasant home, just different. My husband's car was parked outside. It was similar to the one he was currently driving, but looked a little newer. The car I drove up in was new to me as well. The children were not home for some reason. When I came through the door, I found my husband in a big armchair in the family room, fast asleep. I knew that he was home to stay. He was very weary, like he had come home from a long journey. There were no words. I caressed his face. I knew my job was to minister to him and to nurture him as he regained his strength.

Our son had a dream within about a week of mine. He said we were in our house and it was almost his birthday. All four of us were together, and we were talking about putting in a pool. To me, this symbolized light in the darkness, a hope of joyous family time together in the future. I trusted God for what was to come with both of these dreams.

One night that month I went to a pretty intense prayer meeting at the home of my Soul Sister, Lucy. A very anointed woman spoke some prophetic words over my family. She told me I needed to believe God for what He said He would do. She told me to speak to the enemy with force and tell him, in Jesus' name, that he could *not* have my family. She told me she believed God was calling me to a fast. Lucy confirmed by a specific scripture, Hosea 6, how long the fast would be. The prophetess also told me that night to anoint my house with oil—something I did fairly regularly anyway, but she didn't know it. The children and I did anoint our home when we got home that evening. She told me the Lord was saying to get up and pray in those times He wakes me. This is also something I already did, but clearly God knew I was getting weary in this battle. Another word spoken that night was to beware of my children becoming distracted. I knew then that I needed to be more purposeful about us being together, and not be lazy just because I was tired. God was pouring out His Spirit over our family, and I needed to pay attention.

On the way home that evening, I asked God to confirm this word of fasting to me, as I always did. I never took fasting lightly. Also, by that time, I was resisting even the *thought* of a fast, whatever kind it was. That night I had a dream about fasting, where God gave me a specific passage, Matthew 9:14-15. The next morning when I awoke and got in God's Word, this was the very first place I turned to, and not on purpose. I agreed to obey. God also gave me Joel 3:16-18 that next day which declares, "The LORD also will roar from Zion, and utter His voice from Jerusalem; the heavens and earth will shake; but the LORD will be a shelter for His people, and the strength of the children of Israel. So you shall know that I *am* the LORD your God, dwelling in Zion My holy mountain. Then Jerusalem shall be holy, and no aliens shall ever pass through her again. And it will come to pass in that day that the mountains shall drip with new wine, the hills shall flow with milk, and all the brooks of Judah shall be flooded with water; a fountain shall flow from the house of the LORD and water the Valley of Acacias." I knew God was speaking of our restoration here. I was so grateful for His powerful words of promise to me and to my family, even as I continued to wage war in the heavenlies. Meanwhile, here on earth, the Lord was showing me that my husband was continuing in adultery.

The Lord also showed me during this extreme trial that the situation I was currently in was a direct result of my sin of adultery in my first marriage. He gave me Isaiah 40 which explains this concept well. Verses 1-2 state, "'Comfort, yes, comfort My people!' says your God. 'Speak comfort to Jerusalem, and cry out to her, that her warfare is ended, that her iniquity is pardoned; for she has received from the LORD'S hand double for all her sins.'" This is a hard concept for many to swallow. But the God we serve is just. He is holy. He is altogether good. He is miraculous and beautiful and terrible and mighty all at once, and He does discipline those who sin. We do not serve a weak God who has no standards, or who excuses sin. Sin is sin, and it comes with a cost: death.

But our heavenly Father looked down on our frailty after the sin of Adam and Eve and knew that we would all die in our sin, if He did not send us a Savior. So, He lovingly sent us His very own Son to die in our place and to pay the absolute penalty for our sins. *Hallelujah* that we serve a risen Savior, who did not stay in the grave, but raised to life three days later! Our God knew that His Son, Jesus, would be our only hope.

The rest of Isaiah 40 is hopeful, encouraging, and strengthening to God's people. God talks here about making the crooked places straight and the rough places smooth (v. 4). He encourages His children and tells us to lift up our voices with strength, to lift them up and be not afraid because we are beholding our GOD (v.9). He talks of His strength and how He will protect His flock and gently care for those with young (v.10). That was definitely me in that season. At the end of this powerful passage, God speaks of His strength and His infinite understanding and that He is ever present, always with us (v.28). The well-known verses 29-31 declare, "He gives power to the weak, and to *those who have* no might He increases strength. Even the youths shall faint and be weary, and the young men shall utterly fall, but those who wait on the LORD shall renew *their* strength; they shall mount up with wings like eagles, they shall run and not be weary, they shall walk and not faint." Wow. It was really so incredible to me then, as well as now, that the same God who gives us direct and difficult consequences for our sin can be so loving and protecting and nurturing. He truly is our Father. There is no one else who can love us like He does.

One of the important passages God gave me during this season was Hosea 14:4-9 which says (God speaking to Israel), "'I will heal their backsliding, I will love them freely, for my anger has turned away from him. I will be like the dew to Israel; He shall grow like the lily, and lengthen his roots like Lebanon. His branches shall spread; his beauty shall be like an olive tree, and his fragrance like Lebanon. Those who dwell under his shadow shall return; they shall be revived like grain, and grow like a vine. Their scent *shall be* like the wine of Lebanon. Ephraim *shall say*, "What have I to do anymore with idols?" I have heard and observed him. I *am* like a green cypress tree; Your fruit is found in Me.'" I knew the Lord was giving me yet another promise for my husband here, and one that I could personally relate to as well. Clearly this was me at one point; and the Lord had rescued me out of my sin, and redeemed my heart and life. I knew that He was able to do this for my husband as well. And I believed His promise that He would.

December 23rd, 2011, the day after my birthday, the Lord woke me from a dream early in the morning with the words, **"Pray for your family."** I prayed, but kept falling back to sleep. The Lord kept waking me back up in various ways—texts going off, the dog pawing at the bed, the cats nuzzling me, and finally the children awaking. I did finally get up, and He gave me Isaiah 54 to pray over my family aloud, then Isaiah 57:18-19 to pray over my husband. Isaiah 54:5 says, "For your Maker *is* your husband, the LORD of hosts *is* His name; and your Redeemer *is* the Holy One of Israel; He is called the God of the whole earth." Isaiah 54:13 says, "All your children *shall be* taught by the LORD, and great *shall be* the peace of your children." Isaiah 54:17 declares, "'No weapon formed against you shall prosper, and every tongue *which* rises against you in judgment you shall condemn. This is the heritage of the servants of the LORD, and their righteousness *is* from Me,' says the LORD." He was not finished with us yet.

Cindy to Cat 2011

Call those things that are not as though they are. Pray for your husband cover him, your children and your father. Don't take what the enemy is giving you. When the enemy sees you stand and speak God's Word the enemy will be defeated. When God wakes you up, start praying. There are times when you're tired but ask God for strength. You know what I've called you for — ministry. You + your family will redeem many. The enemy has been coming for years +

Lucy's journal pages documenting the prophetic word spoken over me at her home taking little by little. When David was in 2 Kings 7 God said pursue all. I'm standing beside you. This has been overwhelming and the enemy comes in like a flood but we are not fighting for something we are fighting to maintain what God has already given. Strength is coming. The enemy didn't think you would stand + fight. Say ALL IS WELL even when you seem overwhelmed. You will pursue and recover all. No ground will you lose. Speak the word of war over this family. We cover her and her husband, her father with the blood of Jesus. God is the repairer of the breach. We speak restoration + resurrection over the family. We replace every spirit of the enemy with the Spirit of God. Nothing is impossible w/ God. God is going to give you strength and a fight. You have been praying for loved ones and God will bring them to Him. Every knee will bow. 2 Cor. 10 — the rebels are coming back. There is need for your family's vessel. There is work in the Kingdom for your family. There is an end to your torment + trauma. Anoint the door of your house. God is calling you to a fast.

He will give you instructions. He loves you so much and there will be no destruction. The heaviness will lift in the days to come. Perfect love casts out fear. Get ready. We will hear the good report.

CHAPTER 17

"The LORD is my light and my salvation; whom shall I fear? The LORD is the strength of my life; of whom shall I be afraid? When the wicked came against me to eat up my flesh, my enemies and foes, they stumbled and fell. Though an army may encamp against me, my heart shall not fear; though war may rise against me, in this I will be confident. One thing I have desired of the LORD, that will I seek: that I may dwell in the house of the LORD all the days of my life, to behold the beauty of the LORD, and to inquire in His temple. For in the time of trouble He shall hide me in His pavilion; in the secret place of His tabernacle He shall hide me; He shall set me high upon a rock. And now my head shall be lifted up above my enemies all around me; therefore I will offer sacrifices of joy in His tabernacle; I will sing, yes, I will sing praises to the LORD."

~ Psalm 27:1-6

In January of 2012, I realized the word from the Lord for that year was WAIT. He had me waiting everywhere. I waited in the DPS line three different times, two of them for at least two hours apiece. I waited online forever for a repair. I waited in line at J.C. Penney for what seemed like an eternity. I finally asked God, "What is it with all of this waiting?" Then the still, small voice came to my heart, **"You are waiting for ME."** I also realized I was to contact my husband as little as possible during that time—not about money, not about anything. God was my provider now.

Sure, the money still came from my husband most of the time. But he was not my provider. God was. I needed to trust in God and tell Him what I needed. And of course, He already knew. I asked God to help me be a good steward and to stay in His will with the money He provided, and to live well on less if necessary. I felt an enormous amount of peace knowing that HE was my source, and not my husband. This also gave me tremendous freedom to be more peaceful and loving with my children.

I realized I didn't have to be a worry wart. If my bank account was negative and I needed food or *anything* else, instead of being plagued with anxiety and calling my husband and complaining, I just asked God and waited. And He ALWAYS came through for us. It was absolutely incredible, and still one of the best lessons on trust I have learned to this day.

One of my favorite passages, and one God gave me repeatedly then, is 2 Chronicles 20:1-22. At this point in history, the Israelites were facing a grave battle against the Ammonites and the Moabites and some of their rowdy friends. The Bible says King Jehoshaphat of Judah "feared, and set himself to seek the LORD, and proclaimed a fast throughout all Judah" (2 Chron. 20:3). Verse 12 explains their desperation, "'O our God, will You not judge them? For we have no power against this great multitude that is coming against us; nor do we know what to do, but our eyes are upon You.'" Almost immediately, the answer came from God, through His servant Jahaziel. "And he said, 'Listen, all you of Judah and you inhabitants of Jerusalem, and you, King Jehoshaphat! Thus says the LORD to you; "Do not be afraid nor dismayed because of this great multitude, for the battle is not yours, but God's. Tomorrow go down against them. They will surely come up by the Ascent of Ziz, and you will find them at the end of the brook before the Wilderness of Jeruel. You will not need to fight in this battle. Position yourselves, stand still and see the salvation of the LORD, who is with you, O Judah and Jerusalem!" Do not fear or be dismayed; tomorrow go out against them, for the LORD is with you'" (2 Chronicles 20:15-17). The Bible says that the king and all his constituents bowed their faces to the ground and worshipped the Lord right there on the spot. Then on the next morning, they went out singing. That's right. They sent the singers out ahead of everybody else to do battle for them. The Bible says the king "appointed those who should sing to the LORD, and who should praise the beauty of holiness, as they went out before the army and were saying: 'Praise the LORD, for His mercy *endures* forever.'" And then, a magnificent thing happened. As soon as the people began to sing and to praise the Lord, He set ambushes against ALL of their enemies, "and *they were defeated*" (italics mine, 2 Chronicles 20:21-22). Absolutely my favorite part.

On the night of February 16, 2012, I prayed as I was going to sleep and asked God to cover my dreams. When I awoke the next morning, the words, **"Now faith is the substance of things hoped for, the evidence of things not seen"** (Hebrews 11:1) were running through my head. It had been part of my dream, which also included a list of the faith heroes from Hebrews 11. My Soul Sister, Tracy, and her husband were also in my dream, telling me they prayed over their sleep and dreams as well. When I opened my Bible that morning, before I rolled out of bed, I turned straight to Hebrews 11:1, not on my own accord. God was getting my attention yet again.

> Journal entry February 24, 2012:
>
> "Hosea 2-3. Again, God is confirming to me that I am right where I need to be. You told me, Father, at the beginning of this journey, that I was to love my husband as Hosea loved his wife, the prostitute.
>
> I believe God is telling me to begin a marriage healing and recovery ministry (at our church?). I have believed this for some time now, but Linda strongly confirmed it tonight and asked *me* to pray about it. I did, and received a phone call from (friend) relating a story about a marriage healing ministry at our church that had gone awry; and both couples leading are now divorced. Please lead me, Lord. And lead T in this as well, if it is from You."

In March of 2012, while on a retreat in Beaver's Bend with my extended family, God gave me Mark 11:24 which says, "Therefore I say to you, whatever things you ask when you pray, believe that you receive them, and you will have them." He then woke me up to pray on a successive morning, still on the trip, at 4:10 a.m. with our son's alarm, and also at 4:45 a.m. with our niece's alarm, and gave me the verse again. When I went back to sleep eventually, I did so praying for my husband and believing for our marriage. God then gave me a beautiful and loving dream of our healed marriage.

On June 6, 2012, my brother called to tell me of a dream God gave him, where He warned him of something he needed to get rid of in his house. In the dream, God took him to the exact place where the sin-producing thing was. My brother did away with it immediately, knowing His loving God had spared him some heartache. In his dream God had previously shown him a lamp that we grew up with as kids. God showed him that the lamp had a demon attached to it, and He even told my brother the demon's name. My brother called to tell me about it afterward, wanting to warn me about the lamp in case I still had it. I went to sleep that night asking God to please tell me if I still had this lamp in my possession, so that I could do whatever needed to be done.

The next morning, I awoke from a similar dream. In my dream, the lamp was in my upstairs hall closet. Upon rising, I hurriedly went to peruse my hall closet for this lamp. It was not there, but I did find some pictures in an old photo album in a box that I had stashed on purpose, knowing I need not keep them. They were pictures of me doing drugs, smoking and drinking with the old gang. An old friend was in most of them. She had recently died of cancer just the year prior, leaving behind her husband (pictured with us) and two girls. I was saddened as I thought of her and of her family, the direction our friendship had taken, and her tragic end. I threw the pictures out in the trash that morning. It was trash day, and the truck came within the hour. I came back in my house and opened my Bible to Psalm 45. It was a blessing over my life from my Father, the King. Verses 10-11 say, "Listen, O daughter, consider and incline your ear; forget your own people also, and your father's house; so the King will greatly desire your beauty; because He is your Lord, worship Him." Verses 13-14 say, "The royal daughter is all glorious within *the palace*; her clothing *is* woven with gold. She shall be brought to the King in robes of many colors; the virgins, her companions who follow her shall be brought to You. With gladness and rejoicing they shall be brought; they shall enter the King's palace." I just wept.

Journal entry July 6, 2012:

"Romans 8:15-18 'For you did not receive the spirit of bondage again to fear, but you received the Spirit of adoption by whom we cry out, "Abba, Father." The Spirit Himself bears witness with our spirit that we are children of God, and if children, then heirs—heirs of God and joint heirs with Christ, if indeed we suffer with *Him*, that we may also be glorified together. For I consider that the sufferings of this present time are not worthy *to be compared* with the glory which shall be revealed in us.'"

Journal entry July 7, 2012:

"Jeremiah 17:7-8 'Blessed is the man who trusts in the LORD, and whose hope is the LORD. For he shall be like a tree planted by the waters, which spreads out its roots by the river, and will not fear when heat comes; but its leaf will be green, and will not be anxious in the year of drought, nor will cease from yielding fruit.'"

In July of 2012 the children and I took a trip to Mexico with a dear friend (we will call her "Deidra") and her husband and their children. A couple of weeks before we left, when she invited me, she also told me about a new group that she had just joined at her church called Celebrate Recovery. She said people went there to allow God to heal them of all kinds of addictions, and basically any sin patterns. I was intrigued and wanted to hear more. Initially, I thought maybe I would just go with my friend to support her in her efforts toward recovery. Once we were on the trip, she spoke a little more about the group. Her excitement was contagious. I could tell God was doing something really good in her life through this process and through this group. I agreed to check it out at least once for myself.

I ended up inviting my husband on that trip. He surprised the children and I in Mexico, and we had a blast with our friends—only to be let down again when we embarked on U.S. soil and realized nothing else had really changed. He was not ready to come home and live with our family again. I was hurt and angry and felt foolish for allowing him to be a part of our vacation.

Because my husband struggled severely with bitterness and unforgiveness, he often blamed all of our problems on me, telling me I was the reason we were not healed and that he was not ready to come home. I struggled with this lie for a little while, fighting with him at times and trying to reason with him at others, but to no avail. Finally, I gave this lie over to God, who spoke His truth over my life that day in Ephesians 1:4-7 which says, "… just as He chose us in Him before the foundation of the world, that we should be holy and without blame before Him in love, having predestined us to adoption as sons by Jesus Christ to Himself, according to the good pleasure of His will, to the praise of the glory of His grace, by which He made us accepted in the Beloved. In Him we have redemption through His blood, the forgiveness of sins, according to the riches of His grace…." That's Holy Spirit for, **"You don't have any more catching up to do."**

I realized then I would always have changes to make, but as long as I was following Christ, I could continue to remain <u>blameless</u> in Him. He found no fault in me. All my sins were washed away. I had but to confess them to the person I had wronged at the time and then my Lord, and I was forgiven. I had been redeemed. Washed white as snow. So, what was I working so hard at? Who was I working hard to please? I had nothing else to strive to be. I had only to surrender my life to Christ and allow *Him* to change me. When I fell, He would pick me up. He was not standing up there shaking His fist or wagging His finger at me. He *loved* me and was waiting to forgive me when I repented and came back to Him. If my husband chose not to forgive me and wanted to live in the past, so be it. He would be the one suffering under the generational curse of bitterness. I was free in Jesus Christ—set free by *His* blood to live freely in His love.

Psalm 51:7 says, "Purge me with hyssop, and I shall be clean; wash me, and I shall be whiter than snow. Make me hear joy and gladness, *that* the bones You have broken may rejoice. Hide Your face from my sins, and blot out all my iniquities. Create in me a clean heart, O God, and renew a steadfast spirit within me. Do not cast me away from Your presence, and do not take Your Holy Spirit from me. Restore to me the joy of Your salvation, and uphold me *by Your* generous Spirit." Verse 17 states, "The sacrifices of God *are* a broken spirit, a broken and a contrite heart—these, O God, You will not despise." I decided to trust God to do this magnificent work in my life, because He was the only One who could.

And God continued to give me Hebrews 11:1.

I also continued to process what Deidra had explained to me about this Celebrate Recovery group. She said they met once a week on Tuesdays in a share group, and that they were going through a 12-step study. She told me there were only a few more weeks that the class would be "open" before they closed it to new members. Conveniently, for the next couple of Tuesdays (it was one of my husband's nights with the kids), I decided to get my nails done or do something else relaxing, truthfully ANYTHING to avoid actually going to this group. The devil provided lots of excuses. One Tuesday evening, the last one before they closed the group, I was undecided on my relaxing adventure and just asked God to please point me in the right direction. I knew right then He was not going to let me continue to escape. Upon feeling that nudge in my spirit, I turned my car around and headed in the direction of Christ Fellowship Church. When I walked into the portable building in the back, where they held the Celebrate Recovery women's step study, the first thing I said as I was introducing myself was, "I'm just here to observe." My guns were out and loaded. I wasn't prepared to let anyone beyond my guard.

I stayed and listened to these women share their hearts that night. I came back the next week. At that time, the leader said we would all need to find a sponsor to help us through the next phases of our recovery. She explained that an easy way to do this would be to come to the Friday evening support group. There would be many sponsors there—people who had completed the 12 steps and were willing to help others through their recovery. I still didn't even know if this was where I was supposed to be. I was questioning everything and unwilling to commit. I didn't know any of these women. And I didn't really know if I thought this whole process would work for me, or if it was anything I even needed. Why was I even here? I wasn't struggling with drugs or alcohol anymore, and I wasn't a sex addict or even promiscuous anymore. God had completely healed me of those vices.

Nevertheless, I did go to the Friday night group. When I walked into "the Attic" as they called it, I saw a pretty blond woman on stage with a guitar. As she opened our meeting that night, she explained that her name was (we will call her "Jackie") and that she was recovering from anger and from an eating disorder. She had a beautiful voice. As she began to lead us in worship, I knew this woman was my sponsor. All of a sudden, it was like she had a Holy-Spirit halo over her head. Not only did the LORD spotlight her to me as my sponsor, He told me most definitely WHY I was there. Anger. I was there to be freed from the anger that had plagued me since I was a little girl. I couldn't wait to find this woman. I was jumping up and down inside. After the meeting was over, there was a time for refreshments in one of the portables. I was looking for the singing sponsor, but couldn't find her anywhere. I went to the refreshment room and inquired with the woman at the door who was taking donations. Where could I find Jackie? I needed her to be my sponsor, I explained. The woman took my number and said she would give it to Jackie and ask her to call me.

That week Jackie did call me. We spoke briefly, and I shared a little of my story. She said she would pray about whether to be my sponsor and get back to me in a few days with a clear answer. I waited and prayed that God would tell her, "yes," if it were His will, which I definitely believed it was by this time. When she called me back, she said she had not even prayed about it, but that she just knew she was supposed to be my sponsor. I was overjoyed. We agreed to meet weekly by phone, since both of us had pretty tight schedules. I was officially a part of the Celebrate Recovery (CR) program.

One of the most intense parts of the CR program, and the hardest part for most people, is the fourth step called "inventory." Inventory is the weeks-long process of going through a formatted list of questions concerning each unaddressed sin that you either need to ask forgiveness for or to forgive another person for, or sometimes both, and always to take before the Father. There is more than one way to complete this process, and my sponsor had me take the longer, more detailed route. I did not know it at the time, but I would later be grateful for her very thorough instructions for my recovery. Every time I sat down with God to address another sin or hurt before Him, I wept and wept as He unlocked the deepest, darkest parts of my heart and the anguish that I had so neatly tucked away and pretended to deal with all of those years. Decades worth of pain, anger, shame, guilt, thoughts of worthlessness and lies of the enemy came flooding out onto that paper—day after day, week after week. Many weeks and many tear-stained pages later, when my inventory was completed on paper, I sat with my sponsor for hours one afternoon and read this vulnerable mess out loud to her. God could not have picked a more perfect candidate to be my sponsor. Jackie was gentle, understanding and wise, and was with me every step of the way. I felt no criticism or judgment from her as she listened to me read off the list of names I needed to forgive and to ask forgiveness from.

As I continued through the steps, God showed me I had so many more sins I was harboring, so many more lies of the enemy He wanted to break off my life. As several of the Celebrate Recovery teachers explained over that time, these were onion layers that I would continue to allow God to peel off of my life. They were sins and lies that built on each other. Guilt, shame, fear, insecurity, codependency, anxiety. Every time another onion-layer was revealed by God, I could acknowledge it and repent of it, and He could then peel it off. As each onion layer fell to the ground, my spirit soared with the freedom in Christ to be able to acknowledge these sins before the Father and ask Him to take them away from me. I was no longer in hiding. I was finally free. And now I could be free to learn just exactly who it was HE had made me to be in the first place and what my true purpose was in this world.

On November 7 of 2012, my husband and I had a violent fight. He had been talking about coming home again and sort of making some plans, but God continued to show me that he was in adultery. I confronted him one day and he blew up. After this display of violence, I was hesitant to let the children visit with him any more at all. I consulted my Heavenly Father, who took me to 2 Samuel 12-13 which depicts David's children during David's sin and irresponsibility. One child died as a result of his sin. Another was raped because of his irresponsibility. He was often an absentee dad. I had my answer. I texted my husband and told him I did not feel comfortable with him having our kids at all at this time. Then the Lord took me to Isaiah 43 and told me to fear not, because He had redeemed me. He had called me by His name and I was His child. He reminded me that when I walked through the waters, He would be with me, and through the rivers, they would not overflow me. When I walked through the fire, I would not be burned, nor would the flame scorch me, because He was the Lord my God, the Holy One of Israel, my Savior. He gave people for my ransom and to take my place. I had been honored and He loved me (Isaiah 43:1-3). I knew He was protecting my family from further disaster.

On November 14, my husband served me divorce papers. I was cooking dinner and getting the kids and I ready to go to Wednesday night church. Some kid with an evil grin rang my doorbell, then darted into the yard after handing me the subpoena. Shaking, I came back inside and just fell into a ball on the kitchen floor.

I prayed and asked God if I could PLEASE leave my husband now, and if He would please give me a sign that this would be ok with Him. Truthfully, I was so hurt, afraid, confused, tired and angry. I heard nothing.

On November 15, I began interviewing attorneys.

On November 16, I fasted and prayed. I secured an attorney. I chose someone I did not know, but who came highly recommended by many in our community. He was a Christian. When I spoke to him on the phone, he agreed to take the case pro-bono, knowing I had no money to pay. I went to his office to file my case. When the kind paralegal was gathering all my information, she asked me what I wanted out of this divorce. I told her I wanted my husband to come home, and for my family to be saved. I explained that was what God had promised me all along. Bewildered, she asked more probing questions that could give her enough information to do her job. I told her I didn't really know what I was doing there—that I never wanted a divorce—but that since I was there, I guess I wanted to make sure the kids and I had financial security. She took down my information and filed my case with the court.

Journal entry November 16, 2012:

"Psalm 109-111

God is in control. I have been faithful. He will vindicate me. He will gently lead me with my young. He loves us. He is <u>for</u> marriage. I am still praying and believing <u>for</u> my marriage. I believe what my God said. He will repay the years the locusts have eaten. He will open the eyes of the blind. He will heal T and lead him and restore comforts to him and to his mourners. He is coming for me, and for my dear children. He will have His way with my enemies. He is my Father and He loves me with an everlasting love and He is <u>mighty</u> to <u>save</u>. I will yet praise <u>Him</u>.

Psalm 68:12 '…And she who remains at home divides the spoil.'

Psalm 68:5 'A father of the fatherless, a defender of widows, is God in His holy habitation. God sets the solitary in families; He brings out those who are bound into prosperity…'"

Journal entry November 17, 2012:

"Luke 1:46-55, Luke 1:68-75

PRAISE the LORD our GOD!"

On November 17, I received word that a good family friend had died, leaving behind his dear wife, daughter and son. The son had played baseball with our son for years. The man died of unexplained causes. The doctors had been bewildered for months over the many seemingly unrelated health issues that plagued him and finally took his life. He was my husband's age. I emailed my husband to let him know of our friend's death and the memorial service arrangements.

> Journal entry November 18, 2012:
>
> "Isaiah 43 (heart insert).
>
> I have <u>nothing</u> to fear. My Lord has redeemed me and He loves me and has honored me. He is watching over me and will do a new thing, for His glory. He will open the eyes of the blind.
>
> Two days ago, T asked (our son) to have me ask (we will call him "Pastor C"—he was the executive pastor of our church) to call him. Today T told (our son) his car was broken into and his alarm cord cut, and his radio, gun and a cell phone were stolen. When (our son) sent T a picture of (our daughter), he said she looked more and more like me every day."

On Sunday, November 18, the children and I attended the memorial service for our friend. I found myself anxiously looking around during the service to see if my husband was in attendance there. After the service, we went to the fellowship hall to pay our respects to the family. The children and I stood in the receiving line, hugged our friends, and then sat down for a bite to eat. To my surprise at that moment, my husband came ambling over to our table. And then, the Holy Spirit did a miraculous thing. He gave my heart the courage to get up and hug my husband. All of the pain and anger were washed away in a moment by God's forgiveness through me to this man. As I hugged him, he hugged me back. And I could tell it was for real. We both let go of anger and bitterness as we chose love in that moment before God and before our children. My husband sat down with our family, and we conversed lightly before departing our separate ways. He walked us to our car, and we hugged goodbye.

On Monday night, November 19 around 9 p.m., my husband sent me a very long text repenting of his sin, and then asking my forgiveness. He told me he would understand if I chose not to forgive Him, but that He wanted a second chance. He said He was rescinding the divorce proceedings on His end. He said he couldn't believe that the very person he had betrayed, hurt so much, and wronged so deeply could still get up and give him a hug when they saw him. He said that was beyond his understanding, and that he knew it had to be the Lord. I forgave him immediately, knowing full well this was God's plan.

Journal entry November 19, 2012:

"God brought my husband home tonight. He texted me and asked my forgiveness and said he was going to revoke the divorce proceedings. I called him and said, 'Will you come home now?' We talked for over two hours. He is going to read two books[19] Pastor C gave him.* He said he was looking into the *Every Man's Battle*[20] workshop in December in CA. He said he missed his family, not just his kids. He said he'd had to find a house to rent for the kids to have separate rooms for the divorce (per his attorney), and that he'd started thinking about life afterwards with the kids, but couldn't put 'her' in the picture. He knew he still didn't want them to know her. So, he was coming clean. He made a joke and said 'I'm finally growing up, at 40. Think it's too late?' I assured him it was God's perfect year for him. He said he was going to break it off with her, fire her (she was working for our company by this time), revoke the divorce proceedings and unwind the new rent house proceedings. He wanted to come home 'healed,' not 'healing.' My prayer is that he will just come home tomorrow and let <u>God</u> do the rest.

2 Chronicles 16:9 'For the eyes of the LORD run to and fro throughout the whole earth, to show Himself strong on behalf of *those* whose heart is loyal to Him.'

2 Chronicles 17. Jehoshaphat was a <u>good</u> king who fortified the cities and walked in the ways of the LORD and sought GOD and removed the high places and wooden images.

Ezekiel 17-18. God's judgment on His wayward people. His mercy. Setting the captives free. Exalting the lowly and bringing down the proud. Freeing the children from the sins of their fathers. 'Repent and live.'"

The day after my husband's repentance, I called the attorney I had hired and rescinded the divorce. I spoke again with the paralegal who had taken my information in the office. As I explained the miracle that God was working, and told of my husband's repentance the night before, she began looking online at the court filings. Right at that moment, she found our case, and said, "I see right here. This case is dismissed! I just got chills. I believe this is a God thing." I told her to tell me what I owed their firm, knowing their time was worth money. I never received a bill. Months later, I was able to thank this dear lawyer for his kind gesture toward my family.

My husband came home one month later, on December 16, 2012. For good. Emotions ran high in the month before he came home, and there were many loose ends to tie up. At least once, we got into a giant fight over the fact that he still had not fired the woman from our business. But I continued to press in to God, sometimes rather messily, and He continued to forgive me when I was a wreck in His presence, and to love me anyway and guide me on His continual path for His glory. My husband eventually fired the woman, just days before coming home to our family. He then joined a men's Bible study at our new church.

Journal entry December 12, 2012:

"Nehemiah 4:9 'Nevertheless we made our prayer to God, and because of them we set a watch against them day and night.'

I am excited, but this is really hard. T is supposed to be setting up counseling. At times, I just want to run the other way. Good thing I have our kids and some incredible friends to keep me accountable. I know God is doing this. It is just really painful at times, even now. Praying to be aware, for both T and I, of Satan's attacks. Please protect and heal my family, LORD JESUS. I plead the blood of Jesus over my family. We trust You, LORD."

Journal entry December 15, 2012:

"The LORD has healed my precious family. My husband will be home tomorrow. He came to Celebrate Recovery with me tonight. We talked last night for over two hours. This is the second time this week we had a really intimate talk about our relationship based on these questions we are answering in *His Needs, Her Needs*.[21] Very deep, both admitting our wrongs without (much) defensiveness from the other person. Both acknowledging on purpose really important and loving things we could do to meet the other's needs. I am praying to meet his needs. He's been going to the men's *Courageous*[22] Bible study at our church. He is getting involved and he likes it. I am seeing real change. So amazing to watch God work. I am so in awe of You, God, and I love You with all my heart."

**The books mentioned here are* His Needs, Her Needs *by Willard F. Harley, Jr. and* Love and Respect *by Dr. Emerson Eggerichs. They are fantastic tools for any marriage at any stage.*

CHAPTER 18

"Thus says the LORD, who makes a way in the sea and a path through the mighty waters, Who brings forth the chariot and horse, the army and the power (they shall lie down together, they shall not rise; they are extinguished, they are quenched like a wick):

'Do not remember the former things, nor consider the things of old, behold I will do a new thing, now it shall spring forth; shall you not know it? I will even make a road in the wilderness and rivers in the desert. The beast of the field will honor Me, the jackals and the ostriches, because I give waters in the wilderness and rivers in the desert, to give drink to My people, My chosen. This people I have formed for Myself; they shall declare My praise.'"

~ Isaiah 43:16-21

The first year my husband was home with our family was wonderful and completely challenging all at the same time. There was a tremendous amount of spiritual warfare going on. God really impressed upon me the importance of Philippians 4:8 which says, "Finally, brethren, whatever things are true, whatever things *are* noble, whatever things *are* just, whatever things *are* pure, whatever things *are* lovely, whatever things *are* of good report, if *there is* any virtue and if *there is* anything praiseworthy—meditate on these things." He reminded me constantly that as I thought, so I was and would become. Continuing through the process of Celebrate

Recovery and doing daily inventory of my thoughts, feelings and actions truly aided me in this regard. My husband and I counseled for this first year and a half with a godly woman, who came highly recommended by the pastor my husband had confided in.

We also attended Dennis and Barbara Rainey's Weekend to Remember®[23] marriage conference about midway through the year. The Lord continued to tell me to fast quite a bit throughout this first year, alerting me to specifics to pray through for my husband, myself, and our children. God was continuing to break chains off of my family in that year. It sometimes seemed like a very slow process, but God's goals for us are often different than our goals for ourselves. He sees the end goal, and is willing to lovingly and patiently wait for His children to muddle through the long, often painful learning processes that will yield favorable outcomes.

Regarding the woman being fired from our company, it turned out it wasn't as cut and dried as I had originally hoped. My husband ended up hiring an attorney to make sure the whole thing was done properly. That process and the conversations surrounding it were stressful on our marriage. But, when it was completely over, the Lord gave me a dream one night to confirm that chapter in our lives was through. In the dream, I was in a long, dark attic hall. It was dusty and cold. There was an open door in the hallway. I looked into the room to see a kind of daunting, scary mess. The room seemed like it should have been condemned. Then, supernaturally, the door was SLAMMED shut. I awoke from the dream because of the audible slam, which brought me to a start. Heart pounding, I recounted the details of my dream that morning, and realized God was showing me something to get my attention. After journaling the dream, I spent several days seeking to understand what God was saying. I finally realized the dream had come on the night my husband had delivered the news that the attorney had completed the process—all paperwork was signed and the woman was out of our lives for good. I thanked God for always working all things together for our good, and for working miracle after miracle on our behalf.

God kept bringing me women to mentor during this time. He began this process while my husband and I were separated, allowing one woman in my life at a time for at least a year, and bringing me a new friend to walk with each time He brought the previous season to an end. This process of mentoring women was two-fold—not only did God allow my pain to be used for His glory by imparting the wisdom I had gleaned, He also kept me accountable in my own marriage and encouraged me to stay committed in the hard times. The sheer knowledge that someone else was depending on me for their encouragement kept me going at times when I really wanted to bail out.

God also used my children and their sheer well-being to keep me accountable. One weekend, my husband and I were having an especially hard time. This particular day, I was upstairs in the guest bedroom, just sitting on the bed. I was fasting, and I was crying out to God. I was telling Him I couldn't go on like this. I couldn't stomach it anymore. He could just take my husband right back to wherever he was before. I didn't want to do this anymore. As I was having my crying fit with God, right then He opened my spirit eyes to see a quick blip of my children's future, should I choose to take this path and undo all of the work He had done in our family up to this point. It was a flash. I don't really know how to describe it, except that I know it was truth in its entirety. He gave me a vision at that moment of my son and my daughter becoming involved in drugs and promiscuity and just general darkness. He was warning me in no uncertain terms that because of the generational curses which were passed down in our family on both sides, my children would have no future with Christ here on earth, or at least would have years of darkness beforehand, if I chose to disobey my Lord now. Immediately, I knew He was right. I knew in my spirit that, because of my obedience, He was reversing the curses in my family. Indeed, He was single-handedly breaking off the chains that had held us captive for so very long, even for generations. But my faithfulness was not an option. Not anymore—not ever. I repented to Him at that moment and told Him I was all in again, that I was so sorry for my fear and for my selfishness, and that I wanted what He wanted for my family. I told Him I would wait on Him to restore the years the locusts had eaten. I asked Him for strength for the journey. He gave it.

God also took that year to open my eyes to some hard truths about just how codependent I had been in my relationships, especially extended family relationships, up to that point. Through the process of Celebrate Recovery, He showed me that I reacted to pain in some toxic ways, and that I was actually tearing down some of the relationships I wanted to build up, due to my own insecurities. God had me read Cloud/Townsend's book *Boundaries*[24] twice, and make some important changes to some family relationships that extended health and recovery to those involved directly and indirectly. My immediate family would eventually benefit from me learning to say "no" when necessary, and "yes" only when God prompted.

In October of 2013, a year and a few months after I began Celebrate Recovery, I completed my twelve steps. It was time for my graduation ceremony. There I would receive my first "chip," signifying my completion of this program and freedom from my addiction to rage, along with many other spiritual strongholds. I walked across the stage with my dear friend Deidra, both our husbands present. We knew there was no magic formula preventing us from ever sinning in our areas of addiction again. But there was hope. There was a way of escape when the devil continued to tempt us to fall victim to those sin patterns. There were safeguards in place, set forth by the Father, for our freedom to be secure in its boundary of love and hope. There was forgiveness. We were finally free.

In the fall of 2013, I began to realize God's specific call on my life as His "Songbird." I began singing on the praise team with our Celebrate Recovery band, helping to lead worship with my dear friend Deidra at our Friday night group. At the same time, I learned that the place Deidra was taking voice lessons was right in my neighborhood, within walking distance of our home. I began taking lessons as well, as did our son and daughter, and formed a life-long friendship with this special, godly teacher.

And all of that year, over and over again, the Lord gave me Joel 2:25 and told me, ***"I will restore the years the locust has eaten."***

CHAPTER 19

"Two are better than one because they have a good reward for their labor. For if they fall, one will lift up his companion. But woe to him who *is alone when he falls, for* he has *no one to help him up. Again, if two lie down together, they will keep warm; but how can one be warm* alone? *Though one may be overpowered by another, two can withstand him, and a threefold cord is not quickly broken."*

~ Ecclesiastes 4:9-12

In March of 2014 God gave me a prophetic word through a woman I met at a Bible study at our church. This woman has since become a dear friend of mine. We will call her "Sharon." She came up to me and told me I was beautiful, and that the Lord wanted me to know that He loved me very much. She then prayed over me, and said she saw me dancing with Jesus. I was dancing and twirling in to Him and then back out to touch others' lives. She said she saw God doing a great work. She used a term that I forgot to write down, but as I wrote about her in my journal later, the word in my spirit was **"unveiling."** I did feel like we were on the cusp of something huge. Like God's spirit was just taking over and all these promises were unfolding right before our very eyes—everything I had prayed for, and everything the Lord had promised. I knew there was no need for doubt or fear. And as she was praying, Sharon said that I was God's mouthpiece, and that the Lord greatly delighted in me. What a blessing! God knew just how *much* I needed a touch from Him on that very day, and that was clearly a sweet hug from my Lord. He was reminding me of how He truly saw me and how much *He loved* me. The Bible study we were in at the time was a Beth Moore study called *Sacred Secrets*[25] where we were learning about being in the secret with God, working in secret with Him. I went home weeping, because I had been there. I had fought the lion and the bear and cried tears only the Lord knew about. So many times.

And that night God reminded me *I had been* in the secret with Him and done something so amazing with Him—waited for four years on Him, while He gave me promises and daily encouragement and then saved my marriage and my family. Like He'd promised me since at least 2007. Maybe before. The week before had been a nightmare—Satan attacked me with feelings of overwhelming insecurity. However, I discovered as I journaled later that the reason the enemy attacked was because God used me in a very specific way that week—to reveal an important truth to someone who had inadvertently played a role in our story. You see, our trials and God's blessings and His amazing miracles are never just *for us*. There is always a larger story, and many pieces and parts of it unfolding all the time that most of us will never see. Sometimes God gives us glimpses of His working, and that is truly sweet. But I have discovered through trial after trial that God has a great plan, and that my little piece of it is just that—little—compared to His grand story. His main goal is that all hearts are changed and all lives are saved by coming to Him through faith. We won't always know what role we truly play, but our job is to just stay faithful to Him and to plant the seeds He gives us to sow. He waters. He brings the increase.

In May of 2014, my husband began a weekly Bible study, focusing on marriage, at a large church in Dallas. I also noticed him reading his Bible. He began to reach out and talk to other men, encouraging them to stay in their marriages and to not give up. He also began taking a more active role in parenting our children. I was so grateful to see God at work in His life and in all our lives. It was such a great reminder that God is actually ALWAYS at work, often doing things we can't see.

On May 31, 2014, I discovered I was pregnant! I was so excited, I was coming unglued. My husband and children were just as excited as I was. I just felt pure joy. We all felt it.

On July 12, 2014, God took our unborn baby to heaven to live with Him. Losing our baby was devastating to our family, or at least it felt so at the time. Our daughter took it really hard. She was seven years old at the time, and has always had a wisdom beyond her years. We were on vacation with Deidra's family, who had become dear family friends to us. She and her husband were so loving and comforting in our tragic circumstances. Later, we realized we were actually grateful to have been in this place with them when it happened. Nevertheless, I went into a kind of fog afterwards. Post-pregnancy hormones and the traumatic loss created a recipe for depression for me for several weeks, if not months. This was just one of the ways the enemy attacked our family during this season of restoration, and purported the lie that God was not in control. But God continued to send me His love letters and to wrap His loving arms around our entire family. His comfort was enough to sustain us. His goodness was more than enough for us. He gave us His peace in the midst of our storm.

For several weeks toward the end of the year, as I seemed to spiral downward, God gave me the story of David and Goliath in several different ways—in Scripture (1 Samuel 17), in our son's memory verse for school, through a word from my sister as I shared our struggles with her one night. It seemed to be everywhere I turned. Over and over, God kept telling me to face these giants and WIN, with just a sling and a stone and the LORD my GOD. He was going to do it all for me, and my family and I would be victorious in Him, if we would let Him win. Some days I just wept at the thought of His goodness over my family and me in our continued struggle, as we fought against the enemy who attacked our very souls. We were in the fight of our lives now, to keep our family together against all evil attempts to pry us apart again.

The verse the Lord gave me then, through my son, was 1 Samuel 17:45, 47 which says, "David said to the Philistine, 'You come to me with a sword, with a spear, and with a javelin. But I come to you in the name of the LORD of hosts, the God of the armies of Israel, whom you have defied. Then all this assembly shall know that the LORD does not save with sword and spear; for the battle is the LORD's, and He will give you into our hands.'" The verse nestled between those two, 1 Samuel 17:46, declares, "This day the LORD will deliver you into my hand, and I will strike you and take your head from you. And this day I will give the carcasses of the camp of the Philistines to the birds of the air and the wild beasts of the earth, that all the earth may know that there is a God in Israel."

Wow. Pretty, gruesome, right? God knows how to get our attention. He is not weak and He is not playing around with our lives. He is serious about His defeat of our enemies. He *is* our protector. He *is* our mighty defender.

God was doing such amazing things in our lives—it just didn't look like I thought it would. We had so many relationship stressors going on, it was hard to focus on the good that God was doing—which was, of course, the enemy's plan. But as I met with another woman to give her encouragement for her marriage one day that November, I was reminded of the role we play in God's manifest plan. The enemy was prowling about like a roaring lion—not just attacking our husbands, but these "godly" wives as well (1 Peter 5:8). We had to be on our guard against him and to remember that "no temptation" overcomes us except "such as is common to man. But God is faithful, who will not allow you to be tempted beyond what you are able, but with the temptation will always make the way of escape that (we) may be able to bear it" (1 Corinthians 10:12-13). We were constantly at war, and were never to let our guard down. The Lord could, and would, give us His perfect peace in this battle (Isaiah 26:3); but we needed to guard our hearts for Him at all times.

In August of 2014, my husband took our almost twelve-year old son away for a weekend while they went through Dennis and Barbara Rainey's *Passport to Purity*,[26] a Biblical and extremely informative CD series for preteens and their parents. It is a wonderful tool for teaching purity to our youth, while exploring some of the really hard subjects they will undoubtedly experience in the years ahead. They had a good bonding weekend, and I was grateful for my husband's leadership in this effort, knowing our Lord had laid this before us at this time.

And by that November, two years after his repentance, my husband was actively attending our Bible fellowship group at church, the one the Lord had told me to join, as I was kicking and screaming in 2010. He soon joined a Bible study with the men from this group. Our daughter was using her beautiful voice to praise the Lord in the children's choir and sometimes in solo performances at our church. Our son was engaged in the youth group there and loving it. We even signed up that year to host

Disciple Now (D-Now), a weekend where teens are hosted in homes all over the community to learn and grow in Christ, as they participate in all kinds of fun events and worship. God was orchestrating every part of it, teaching my husband to lead and me to follow, and our family just to trust in Him with our very lives.

CHAPTER 20

"Be in pain, and labor to bring forth, O daughter of Zion, like a woman in birth pangs. For now you shall go forth from the city, you shall dwell in the field and to Babylon you shall go. There you shall be delivered; there the LORD will redeem you from the hand of your enemies."

~ Micah 4:10

2015 was an extremely difficult year. Our daughter wrote in her "I Have a Dream" project for school that her dream for her family was that her parents would not fight all the time. All our hearts were hurting; and there was virtually no good communication happening between my husband and me. There was plenty of the other kind. I began to realize that my role in this fight for our family at this point was to release my husband to the Lord and to speak only when God told me to, but then definitely to speak the words that He gave me to speak. In other words, I needed to be tuned in at all times.

Meanwhile, God had been showing me for the last couple of years that we now had two strong-willed children. While this temperament, referenced by Dr. James Dobson in his books *The Strong-Willed Child*[27] and *The New Strong-Willed Child*,[28] is actually a blessing as children grow into adulthood and is present in many adult Christian leaders, it is difficult to deal with when children are young. And when they are faced with a familial disaster like the one we had been through, parenting can feel hopeless. At times I definitely felt I was doing it alone, since my husband was apparently processing something with God during this year that I could not help him with. My job was to pray and to stay out of the way. We definitely were not harmonious. There were arrows and darts flying all around us. God was our only hope, and staying in His Word was my only sanity—and sanctity. At times, I questioned the decision we made to rekindle our relationship, telling God I did not feel we were fit as parents to be raising these dear children. I felt we were doing them more harm than good in our current state. Most of this year I just wanted to put my head under a pillow and not come out until it was all over.

Thankfully, in March of that year, God gave me the opportunity to write Bible studies and do some blogging for an online ministry, as their Director of Training. This position was fruitful for me in that it unleashed the passion God had given me to share some of the wisdom He had placed deep within me. As I continued to lead others in worship by singing on the praise team at Celebrate Recovery, mentoring women and now writing, I was beginning to feel like I had a voice. I could feel God awakening these gifts that He had determined for me since the beginning of time.

That year, the Lord gave me the story of parting the waters, the Red Sea and the Jordan River.

>
> Journal entry June 4, 2015:
>
> "The remedy to the fear, anger, anxiety, and depression I struggle with is praise. Isaiah 61. He will give me the garment of praise for the spirit of heaviness."
>
> Journal entry June 7, 2015:
>
> "I am trusting the LORD for this fresh word for my family. He is rolling back the waters of the Jordan River until we have crossed over. We will conquer the lands He has given us. We will find our victory in Him. We will set up memorial stones to Him, that we and our descendants may always remember the amazing power, love and grace

of the LORD our God. He is mighty to save. Help us to have courage, LORD, and not be afraid."

Journal entry June 23, 2015:

"Exodus 14-15

Praising the LORD for rolling back the Red Sea and the Jordan River. Thanking Him in advance for the healing that I know has already taken place in my husband and in our family in God's eyes. It is already done. God has seen what I cannot see, and I believe that it is already done. I have slept upstairs for the past two nights. God has told me to separate from Tim. Obadiah 13, Isaiah 51-52. I labored over what that truly meant and even told T he needed to leave, or that the kids and I would go to a shelter. But upon further review, I don't have a real peace about that. I believe this (being upstairs presently) is where God wants me for now, until He parts the Red Sea and the Jordan River completely, and we can walk through on dry ground—the horse, chariots, riders and Pharaoh thrown into the sea."

In July of that year, a good friend whose Bible studies I had been attending asked me to step in and lead in her absence. She encouraged me to be led by the Spirit and prepare to be flexible. I did pray to hear and obey God's voice in my teaching, and on the morning of the Bible Study felt God leading me to share my testimony instead of the lesson I had prepared. I shared, focusing mainly on my own personal testimony of how God had brought me to Himself, with just snippets of things we'd gone through in our marriage. It was rough. I felt awkward and embarrassed afterward, and felt that I had shared too much. But as I let the Holy Spirit heal me through that, I realized He was proud of me, and that I had glorified Him—even if only a handful of women's hearts were touched—or even just one or two. His goal was not about quantity as much as about quality, and He showed me that if one heart was mended that day from the pain the enemy had caused, then it was well worth my boldness.

In October, God used our daughter to sing at a fundraising event to benefit unborn babies and their mamas who may have been contemplating abortion. She was slated to sing a solo verse of "All the Poor and Powerless"[29] with the praise band. The enemy attacked her for a solid ten days prior to the benefit with a nasty virus. The evening of the event, she sang her heart out while battling a fever of 102 degrees. She truly sounded like an angel. God is *mighty* to save and was making our girl an overcomer in the strongest sense of the word.

In that same month, God showed me that He was teaching our son to run for Him. He began running cross country that year. I had known since he was three that God made him to be a runner. But as I ran with him one weekend through the hills of Austin, God showed me (and I told him!) he had the heart of a lion. He was strong, yet gentle at times, and he would overcome mightily in Jesus' strength. He was a leader and a protector. God had given him a valiant heart.

The hits just kept on coming for our family that year, though. My husband's business was undergoing some change, and he was frustrated. During that time, we had to install two brand-new air-conditioning units in our home. Then we had a flood upstairs. We discovered that the two toilets upstairs had been leaking into the ceiling for at least one year. We had some new flooring installed in the bathrooms the year before, and the contractor didn't lengthen the pipe under the toilets to accommodate the thicker floors. We had the mold experts out to dry everything; then a construction crew cut two giant holes in the ceiling under those toilets, finally installing new sheetrock. But God was faithful. He kept speaking His truths over me and over my family, like Psalms 139-142, telling me I was fearfully and wonderfully made and that He was defeating all of my enemies. He also gave me I Corinthians 9:10 which says, "…he who plows should plow in hope, and he who threshes in hope should be partaker of his hope." He was constantly encouraging me to persevere in this battle, to be an overcomer, and to never stop believing in Him for the miracles He had promised.

Journal entry October 22, 2015:

"Romans 8:16 'The Spirit Himself bears witness with our spirit that we are children of GOD.'

Romans 8:35-39 'Who shall separate us from the love of Christ? *Shall* tribulation or distress or persecution or famine or nakedness or peril or sword? As it is written, *"For Your sake we are killed all day long; we are accounted as sheep for the slaughter."* Yet in all these things we are more than conquerors through Him who loved us. For I am persuaded that neither death nor life, nor angels nor principalities nor powers, nor things present nor things or come, nor height nor depth, nor any other created thing shall be able to separate us from the love of God which is in Christ Jesus our Lord.'"

At the end of October, God called me out of the online ministry. He showed me some Biblical discrepancies that were taking place, and then used me as a watchman to confront the leadership, speaking the truth in love. After weeks of prayer and discernment, and then taking another party with me to confront the leadership as the Bible dictates, God called me out of the ministry when it was obvious no real changes would be made. Nevertheless, I was extremely grateful to have had this opportunity to learn and grow in the Lord.

God showed me through my mentor, Linda, that year that *I was* His Zerubbabel. One day as we were sitting together at the Dallas Arboretum, she took out an article she had been wanting me to read. In it, the author was calling the reader to "be God's Zerubbabel."[30] The Holy Spirit hit me with it then and there. That was what He had been saying to me all along.

God knew I was still waiting on Him for some major breakthrough in my marriage. One morning in early November, I awoke to the words, **"The King's heart is in the hand of the LORD, like the rivers of water; He turns it wherever He wishes"** (Proverbs 21:1).

Journal entry November 6, 2015:

"Isaiah 43

Isaiah 60:22 '"A little one shall become a thousand, and a small one a strong nation. I, the LORD will hasten it in its time."'

Claiming this for my children. And also Isaiah 61:4-7 'And they shall rebuild the old ruins, they shall raise up the former desolations, and they shall repair the ruined cities, the desolations of many generations. Strangers shall stand and feed your flocks, and the sons of the foreigner *shall be* your plowmen and your vinedressers. But you shall be named the priests of the LORD, they shall call you the servants of our GOD. You shall eat the riches of the Gentiles and in their glory you shall boast. Instead of your shame *you shall have double honor,* and *instead of* confusion they shall rejoice in their portion. Therefore in their land they shall possess double; everlasting joy shall be theirs.'"

On December 2, 2015, I awoke from a dream in which our son was telling me, in a more grown-up voice than he currently possessed, that he would awaken at 5. I heard his voice, and it woke me up. I went back to sleep and got up at 6 a.m., when my alarm went off. I walked out of our bedroom and into the dark family room, where I was startled to hear him say, "Good morning." He told me he had arisen a little after 5 to have his quiet time.

The morning before, I was also awakened from a dream in which I heard someone calling my name. I know now that God had us so tightly in His grip, and He was letting me know He had it all under control. Everything I had been and was praying over my family—He had us all in the palm of His hand. He would never let us go, and no one could snatch us out of His hand.

CHAPTER 21

"...therefore choose life, that both you and your descendants may live; that you may love the LORD your God, that you may obey His voice, and that you may cling to Him, for He is your life and the length of your days; and that you may dwell in the land which the LORD swore to your fathers, to Abraham, Isaac, and Jacob, to give them."

~ Deuteronomy 30:19-20

The year 2016 was full of promise and blessing. It also presented its challenges, but not nearly as many as the year before. Our daughter was baptized that year by our pastor, with her daddy in the water by her side. Our family joined us for this joyous occasion, and God used it to encourage us all in our obedience to Him. He was still healing us, still continuing to restore the years the locusts had eaten.

In January of 2016, I left the Celebrate Recovery praise team and joined the worship team at our church. I felt God strongly calling me to make this change at this time. I was very grateful for all God had done in my life through my time with Celebrate Recovery. Now this season was over, and a new one was beginning. I knew God was calling my family and me to some key missions in our church. Through beginning my journey with the Worship and Arts ministry at this time, God continued opening my eyes to more of my spiritual gifting and to specific ways I would be used in His Kingdom for His glory.

In February of 2016, I began leading a women's marriage-intensive study (a morning and an evening group to accommodate working wives) that would last for most of the year. This was in obedience to a prompting from the Lord. My Texas Mama, Linda, had given me *The Power of the Praying Wife*[31] book and study guide the month before as a Christmas gift. She made sure I understood it was not just a gift, but she believed God showed it to her in the bookstore with my name on it. She said she believed I was supposed to lead women in a study on marriage. I prayed for confirmation right there in her living room, but I already knew.

In March of 2016, our family joined a group led by some dear friends going to the Dominican Republic on mission. There was much spiritual warfare surrounding that trip, but God was mighty to break through every attack and scheme of the enemy. We definitely grew in the Lord by leaps and bounds on that trip, even including a time when my husband led a devotional for our group one evening.

> Journal entry from the plane ride home, March 16, 2016:
>
> "Oh! (Our son) led (a boy at the batey, we will call him 'Stephen') to Jesus one morning as we were passing out the EvangeCubes®.[32] We were explaining the cubes to the people while (we will call her 'Donna') was translating. All the while, (our son) was going through the instructions in Spanish and reading the explanation of the cube to little Stephen on his lap. Before we were finished, he started saying, 'Mom! Stephen just accepted Jesus in his heart!' Not wanting to interrupt the teaching, I quieted him down. He began telling A (friend), out of pure excitement. Again, I tried to quiet him to 'wait' for the right time. He whispered to me, 'Mom, I read the whole thing to him in Spanish and then asked him (in Spanish) if he wanted to invite Jesus to be his Savior at the end, and he said, "Yes!"'" (Our son) prayed with Stephen the 'sinner's prayer' on the EvangeCube® sheet and Stephen asked Jesus into his heart. I began to realize that what he was saying and doing was like Mary while I was being like Martha. I am *so* proud of that kid. I knowingly loved on him with my eyes, while

the teaching was coming to a close. I then congratulated him and Stephen and welcomed Stephen into God's, and our family. Then, as the craft was starting, it hit me. I needed to be doing the same thing with whoever the LORD brought me! I turned to (our daughter), who was playing with (her new Haitian friend at the batey; we will call her 'Maria'). I asked them to come sit on the ground with me. I quickly grabbed (friend from the batey; let's call her 'Monique') as well, and sat both girls on my lap while (our daughter) sat next to me and held the cube and turned it at appropriate times. Praying as I read the entire explanation in Spanish, I trusted God to do the rest. At the end of the explanation, I asked Donna to come over to make sure I'd done it right. She showed me the right question to ask. We asked Monique, who said she was already a Christian (praise the LORD!). Then we asked Maria. She said she wanted to receive Jesus in her heart! I asked her again to make sure she understood. Agh! The perils of being a grown-up. She said yes again. I prayed the prayer with her. She understood every word, as she was repeating the prayer out loud while I was praying it in my broken Spanish. What an amazing day and an amazing miracle GOD allowed our family to be a part of. Both of my children being part of (and leading) children to Christ. I was (and am) overjoyed. I hugged both Maria and Monique and congratulated Maria on being a member of God's family now! I am still amazed as it is coming to me in waves—the goodness of the LORD and what He allowed our family to be a part of on this trip.

I am so proud of both our children. (Our son) instantly went in and got acquainted with the kiddos and played with everyone and loved on them in his all-out style. No one is a stranger to him. But even more so than he would at home with a group of kids he didn't know; he was just instantly at home. He made dear friends, hopefully friends for life. If the LORD wills, we will continue to go back. I will definitely continue to pray.

(Our daughter) hung back a little at first, but still interacted with all the kids and got involved. The LORD just led her and strengthened her, and she jumped in, even though it wasn't as much in her comfort zone. But about day three, maybe four, she'd met Maria, who stuck by her side, and (our daughter) by hers, throughout the remainder of our time together.

And (we will call him 'Julian'). He was a little (4?) year-old boy with a great big heart and a great big smile. He won my husband's, and soon all of our hearts right away. Immediately, when T met Julian, he began holding him and carrying him around wherever he went. (I thought we were going to talk about adoption before the trip was over!) Really heart touching."

Journal entry from March 16, 2016:

"P.s. (Our son) said in the car on the way home from the airport that he would have slept at any of their houses, if they asked him to. Yesterday afternoon and evening he was really depressed because we weren't still there. When I came and sat by him and told him I understood and that I was sorry, he began to cry. He loves this people so much. I believe God did a great work in his heart through this trip, and that He is showing him and us that (our son) has a calling to the mission field. At bedtime, he prayed and thanked God for moving in his spirit and for changing his heart and filling his soul. He asked Him to continue to change his heart for Him. What an incredible gift we have been given. I told him I really believed this may be God showing us his calling in life. I also told (our daughter) at bedtime that I was so proud of her for how she just jumped in at the batey, even though she didn't know what to do, and did what she knew how to do until she felt more comfortable. She was so strong and flexible and a real asset on this trip. I love my kiddos!"

That summer, our children attended Sky Ranch as they had been doing since our son was eight years old. It was the third year for our daughter and the seventh year for our son to go. God kept growing them by leaps and bounds there. Our daughter overcame great fear by the power of the Lord that summer, and ended up getting the "Steadfast Heart" award because her love for Jesus just shined through the entire week. Her counselors told us she made so many friends in the cabin, and that she was such a leader. They told us there was even an argument about her being able to have more than one friend, because at least one girl wanted her all to herself, but that it was a great teaching time. When we picked her up, she just cried and cried because she wanted to stay with her new friends! Our son stayed two weeks that year, and was in the leadership portion of the camp by that year, because his aim was (still is) to be a camp counselor when he was old enough. His counselors gave him the "Mighty Man" award for being such a leader in everything, and for shining for Christ with his joyful spirit. I was, and continue to be, so amazed at the beautiful blessings the Lord bestowed on us in these children, even with the constant trials in our marriage. He was and is such a loving and miracle-working God.

In July of 2016, I began to hear the Lord's voice about moving to the country. After praying intensely about it and discussing it with my husband (and children), we began the process of putting our home on the market and looking at rural properties, particularly in Celina which I had heard from the Lord. I had my real estate license by this point, an act of obedience to the Lord in 2012, so that side of it was easy because we didn't have to involve a third party. More on this later.

In November of that year, our family took a trip to Curacao, a Dutch island in the Southern Caribbean Sea. We had been traveling a great amount since my husband had arrived home. I believe that purpose was two-fold. My husband wanted to celebrate us all being back together; and God showed him during our time apart that all the traveling he was doing for work would have been much more enjoyable with his family. I believe the second reason is that it was the great escape. When we were away, the hope was that we could alleviate some of the stress and hard work of trying to put this marriage back together. I will say that each of the trips we took was a good escape for a little while. But by the time the trip was over, we often realized it was just as much (if not more) hard work being on vacation, because we couldn't escape each other when we were frustrated! But this particular trip, this Thanksgiving of 2016, God used to open my eyes to what He was truly doing. He told me not to thwart the process—that He was taking the time we were spending away, each time in a beautiful or definitely interesting setting, to do some "intensives" on us. So, I could either get on board, or I could balk at the whole process. I chose to get on board. By the end of that Thanksgiving trip, God was showing me some important truths about *myself* that weren't so pretty to see and that definitely needed to change. I will describe below.

Journal entry November 28, 2016:

"I learned a lot this past week about myself, and my marriage and my family. I'm going to try and remember it all and write it down. Please help me, Lord.

I learned I can be kind of annoying. Because of stress (anxiety, insecurity), sometimes I blurt things out without thinking or in a disorderly fashion or just don't stay focused. I'm asking God to help me with this. I see it as stressful to my marriage and to T, but also to my kids and other people. God, please help me to be calm and listen more than I speak and to speak Your words.

I learned that I try to take over. I often hear what T has said and disregard it and try to correct him and give him my truth or the "right" answer. Yikes. Ouch. This hurts. I pray, Lord, for a humble spirit, that I will hear <u>Your</u> truth (which is the only truth), and will respect my husband

and the brains and experience You have given him, and his position of authority under God.

I learned that I am highly critical of T a lot of the time. My thought life is <u>not</u> pretty sometimes. I had to continue repenting to the Lord this week and asking Him to remove criticism from my thoughts and to replace it with grace and humility. I now pray the same, Lord, and ask that You help love to be above all."

Journal entry November 29, 2016:

"I also learned that T and I both still treat each other as if we know what the other will do or say, based on the past. This leaves no room for growth or for God to move on our behalf. Our whole family suffers as a result.

God, please help T and I to see ourselves and each other through Your eyes, admitting that we are not mind readers, nor can we tell the future. Help us to remember that acting or reacting negatively to someone or something because of something we propose or suspect about the future is acting ignorantly. Help us to treat each other with dignity, respect and love because we believe and trust in a God who loves us and who is for us and who *moves mountains* on our behalf. In Jesus' name I pray, amen.

I also learned that we both still struggled with the pain of rejection, and actually that defensiveness against rejection does run in our family lines. We often treat each other accordingly, having misunderstandings based on anticipating rejection from the other. In turn, we often reject the other as a defense mechanism! Ahhgh! What a vicious cycle. Father, I pray that T and I will treat each other with love and in humility and walk in accordance with Your truth over our lives. In Jesus' name, amen. I pray this over (our son and our daughter) and any future descendants we have as well, in Jesus' name! Amen."

Journal entry December 1, 2016:

"Jeremiah 20:9b 'But *His word* was in my heart like a burning fire shut up in my bones; I was weary of holding it back, and I could not.'"

Journal entry December 2, 2016:

"Confessions made to T of all the Lord revealed on our trip. God guided my words and his response, as I prayed He would. I also have continued to anoint his feet with oil occasionally at night while he sleeps and to pray over him. Trusting God to continue breaking down these walls and strongholds as only He can!

Also, two nights ago (Tuesday night), T had a dream. Gangsters were attacking our family with guns and knives. He rescued us as best he could, but at times it seemed his efforts were of little use and not prevailing. By the dream's end, the men were in handcuffs and being taken away by the police. It was only then that T could let down. He began to realize the emotion of what had happened. He angrily yelled at the men, 'You tried to take (hurt?) my family!' and then broke down crying. He was blown away by the impact of the dream and couldn't wait to tell me the next morning.

I am confessing my sins now to the Lord, after confessing them to T. I am asking Him to heal our family and to help us walk in love, joy, peace, patience, kindness, goodness, faithfulness, gentleness, and self-control. Also asking God that we would walk in forgiveness and truth and humility and wisdom. In Jesus' name, LORD, let it be! Amen."

Journal entry December 3, 2016:

"We are going to plant a tree in our backyard on December 16 this year, the anniversary (four years) of T's coming home.

'…that they may be called trees of righteousness, the planting of the LORD, that He may be glorified' (Isaiah 61:3).

—from the LORD for me (our family) in my spirit yesterday as He solidified the 'tree planting' in my heart. I love You, Abba. I don't deserve Your love for me."

Journal entry December 27, 2016:

"We are having a beautiful Christmas season, full of peace and love and the joy of the Lord. We planted our Live Oak tree in the backyard on Christmas Eve day in honor of T coming home to our family in December 16th, four years ago (2012). We hosted my dad's side of the family Christmas Eve and Christmas morning—19 for dinner (including two work friends and one of their sons), and then my family spent the night. T's family came too. There was peace and love and harmony and joy.

T gave me a trip to Italy for Christmas. We leave February 9th. I am still blown away. I have prayed since 2010, when I worked market for (a showroom at the World Trade

Center) in August or October that we would get to go to Italy, specifically Tuscany, where we are staying, for a second honeymoon. I know I have mentioned it a couple of times over the last six years, but not a lot. T didn't seem to remember at all that I specifically wanted to go, when I asked him on Christmas day how this came about. He just said M (friend) told him about a deal he couldn't refuse. GOD is so truly magnificent. I can't wait to see what He has planned for us!

And you shall 'be called trees of righteousness, the planting of the LORD that He may be glorified' (Isaiah 61:3).

"'For I know the plans I have for you," declares the LORD, "plans for good and not for evil, to give you a future and a hope"' (Jeremiah 29:11).

'For since the beginning of the world men have not heard nor perceived by the ear, nor has the eye seen any God besides You, who acts for the one who waits for Him' (Isaiah 64:4)."

On December 30, all the Soul Sisters came to our house for the day. Five women and sixteen children, ranging in age from two months to fourteen years of age (my husband was working that day). We had a ball. We loved on each other and commemorated the year by talking of all of God's blessings and the hope that He continued to bestow on all of our families. In the evening, Lucy and her family remained. We prayed for each other and for our families. While she prayed for our daughter, and specifically over her as she slept in her bed, the Lord gave her a vision of an angel standing floor to ceiling in her room, the very room where both our children were sleeping (they had changed rooms by this time) when the Lord gave me the original vision of the angels standing guard over our children, standing floor to ceiling. When she told me, I said, "I know," with a loving smile. When she then prayed over our son, she also saw a floor to ceiling angel in his room. I could barely contain my excitement and awe as I described my similar vision to her from years ago. The next day, Lucy called me with a postscript to the visions she'd described the day before. The angel she had seen in our son's room was "chillin'" on his windowsill. The angel in our daughter's room was a warring angel.

CHAPTER 22

"Arise, shine; for your light has come! And the glory of the LORD is risen upon you."

~ Isaiah 60:1

In January of 2017, God instructed me to participate in a church-wide Daniel fast that would begin that month. For those who don't know, a Daniel fast is a 21-day fast from pleasant foods (meat, milk, honey, anything processed). Again, the sole purpose of any fast is to press in to God, simply by the sheer physical posturing of giving something, or some things, up in order to focus more closely on Him. His heart is often supernaturally revealed to the believer who is pressing in to Him in this way. During that 21-day journey, God very clearly spoke to me about writing this book, among other things. I knew it was time to start, and I was obedient.

In February, my husband and I went to Italy on our second honeymoon, as promised by God. It was an intimate and sweet trip, and very good for our marriage. God absolutely knew what He was doing, and it didn't come a moment too soon! We were grateful for the reprieve and the time away to be reminded of why we fell in love in the first place. God planned the entire trip too, giving us specific places to visit that were often surprises as we went along! For instance, we just "happened" upon Leonardo da Vinci's home and the town bearing his name, nestled up in the Tuscan mountains just behind where we were staying. I will forever remember that sweet gift from God, and from my husband.

Also in February, upon returning from our trip, my marriage-intensive groups started up again and continued through most of the year. That season we studied *Created to Be His Help Meet*. This was one of the things God said to me on our family's trip to Curacao the Thanksgiving before. As I prayed then and asked for His leading concerning these groups, He clearly spoke this book as the focus of our next study. I began to realize while leading these studies, that this initiative from God was again two-fold. Not only was I encouraging other women in their marriages by my testimony and with these studies, but I also remained accountable to them as we continued to be transparent and to lift each other up in prayer for our marriages. This was a complete strengthening tool for me and for my family. Many days, weeks, and months may not have gone the way they did, except as a result of these studies and these friends holding each other accountable.

In July, God took us on another family vacation, full of learning and blessings galore.

Journal entry July 30, 2017:

"We come home from our St. Maarten vacay tomorrow. We have had a miraculous trip. God has protected us and grown us in a myriad of ways. We have had several good 'discussions' but no fighting. We have had godly parenting lessons, good communication, (intimacy), family bonding, marriage strengthening, growth, harmony and T leading.

So grateful to GOD for the ways He is breaking through in my husband's life and for our family.

Continuing to pray His protection and healing and strengthening over my family. Continuing to glorify Him and HIM alone for His miracles and the promises He alone fulfills for my family!!! I love You, Abba!!!"

Journal entry July 31, 2017:

"Leaving Sint Maarten today.

2 Kings 6:16-17 'So he answered, "Do not fear, for those who *are* with us *are* more than those who *are* with them." And Elisha prayed, and said, "LORD, I pray, open his eyes that he may see." Then the LORD opened the eyes of the young man, and he saw. And behold, the mountain *was* full of horses and chariots of fire all around Elisha.'"

My husband and I were dating each other again by this time. God had provided many opportunities for us to just steal away and have an evening together, and we were beginning to really understand the importance of doing just that. In August, we went on a trip to New York together for a few days as part of a gift I had given my husband for Christmas. God continued to work on our relationship during that time, while insuring our children were safe at home with my mother-in-law.

In October of 2017, I was asked to write the budget letter for our school that would go out to all the families. I knew that this was God's cue saying, **"Go. Now is the time to tell them what I have done for you."** I was so grateful for the opportunity to glorify Him for all He had done in our family, in the eleven years we had been at our school.

In November of that year, the Lord gave me a sweet kiss from heaven. My journal excerpt will probably describe it best.

Journal entry November 9, 2017 (as I am writing this book, I am just realizing this is almost nine years to the day that my husband left):

"I led worship again today! It was exhilarating. I felt God's presence almost constantly. And so much freedom. There was some fear a couple of times; but God abolished it, and He brought my voice out for HIM.

Then tonight, after (our son's) XC (Cross Country) banquet, which was so meaningful and wonderful and fulfilling God's promises in our lives of restoring the years the locusts have eaten in so many ways—I am so proud of that boy and all of his hard work and for the faithful young man that he is truly becoming—I met (dear friend, we will call her "Tabitha") at this (church) conference where a man who sees in the Spirit was speaking. He talked about seeing God's face. He then asked us to close our eyes and prayed over us for vision, seeing in the Spirit from God. I prayed that no one would touch me or prophesy over me unless it was from God. I also told God I did not need to see His face unless He wanted to show it to me. But that I just wanted more of Him. I prayed to hunger more for Him. What I did see was the lion in my dream from when I was a young girl. That lion is the best representation of God I have felt. God gave me that very real dream of being embraced by the lion to fully represent Himself to me. That lion was (is) my protector, my best friend, my comfort, my nurturer, my playmate. He loved me; and I felt warm and strong in His embrace. I felt that way on the platform today. Warm and strong and free in His embrace. I felt loved. In my dream, I felt so much love. Tonight, my friend (we will call her "Sarah;" she worked at the place where the meeting was being held. I didn't realize who she was until she came to pray) prophesied over me. She said she saw smoke rising from my head. The Lord showed her it was Frankincense. The Lord showed her I had made great sacrifices of praise and sacrifices with my life. He told her I was so precious to Him, and that my sacrifices were precious. (Sarah was not someone I knew well, and she definitely had no way of knowing these details about my life.) Wow. God continues to anoint my head with oil in a dry and thirsty land. I do <u>not</u> deserve Your love for me, Abba Father! I love You with <u>all</u> of my heart! I also realized I needed to put the lion dream in my book! Somewhere toward the beginning. I can't wait to write about it. I love You, Lord, with <u>all</u> of my heart! You know my every move! You watch my every step."

Also, there were other sacred nuggets from God to keep me going.

Journal entry November 14, 2017:

"I love You Jesus, my Jesus. I know You see me and my sacrifice of praise. I am eternally grateful for that <u>word</u> from <u>You!</u>

(Our daughter) is now reading God's Word to put herself to sleep. The LORD prompted me, and I suggested it yesterday. She read until 9 last night, going to bed at 8 p.m., and had a story to discuss with me this morning! (It was about Lot and the angels and his daughters in Sodom and Gomorroh!)"

Journal entry November 18, 2017:

"Hosting D-Now for our 4th year in a row! We have seniors this year, and (our son) is participating as a 9th grade high school student. Expecting God to do BIG things—it has been a <u>week</u> of breakthrough (Sunday) followed by <u>many</u> spiritual attacks.

God is so completely amazing. God keeps giving me the word, *'veil'* lately.

I love You, LORD, and I praise Your holy name!!! Forever and ever I will praise you and live out the sacrifice of praise!"

Journal excerpt from November 25, 2017:

"Yesterday morning God reminded me as I stood in front of the mirror getting ready that He absolutely can and <u>will</u> use me—despite my faults and flaws—as He used Bathsheba, Rahab, and Mary Magdalene (who I often equate myself with these days). I know my sacrifice of praise is precious—it is Frankincense to my Savior, as Mary's (or the woman in the Bible that some say is Mary Magdalene) alabaster flask of Spikenard oil was precious to Jesus. Mary knew the good part. I want to sit at Jesus' feet."

Journal entry November 28, 2017:

"Yesterday I read again about the *veil* being removed in *Seeking Allah, Finding Jesus*.[33]

On p. 154, Nabeel writes, 'It was as if, rather suddenly, a *veil* (italics mine) of certainty was lifted and I was seeing the potential of the world in a new light. It was like I had been wearing colored glasses my entire life and they had been taken off for the first time. Everything looked different, and I wanted to examine it all more carefully.'"

Journal entry December 2, 2017:

"Lamentations 2:19

I am to pour out my heart like water before the face of the LORD and lift up my hands toward Him for the lives of my young children. I am praying for (our son and daughter) to put all distractions aside and to seek the LORD and then to find Him when they have sought Him with all their hearts. I am praying for them to hunger and thirst for His Word.

Psalm 40

I am continuing to pray that God will use me, use T, use (our son and daughter) to stand on whatever platform He would place us on for His glory and to speak His truth to our church, other churches and to the nations."

Journal entry December 25, 2017:

"On Christmas Day, Jesus <u>kept</u> speaking to me about the fellowship of suffering. How He was <u>not</u> esteemed or recognized when He came into this world, unto His own! They esteemed Him not. He was crucified and died for <u>my</u> sins! And thank Him and praise His holy <u>name</u> that He rose again!!!"

Journal excerpt from December 27, 2017:

"I Samuel 1:27-28

The Lord took this morning to remind me that because of my obedience, even through the fiery trials, my children are safe with Him and have been lent to the LORD (they are already His) as long as they live."

Sadly, very shortly after the Lord gave me the powerful prophetic word in November, the enemy took me down a path that deterred my thinking and endangered my family. I let my guard down for a moment, and destruction almost prevailed. I did discuss these thoughts, and the actions they provoked, with my husband and asked his forgiveness. He gave it. I repented to the Lord and received His forgiveness. The story that comes to mind is Peter in the courtyard, denying Jesus three times, immediately after He told Jesus He would never be made to stumble, and that he would die with Him before he denied Him (Matthew 26:33-75). But the next story I remember is the one of Jesus cooking Peter breakfast over a coal fire, after Jesus had risen from the grave (John 21:1-19). He asked Peter three times if he loved Him. Peter insisted, almost heartbroken by the third prompting, that he loved Jesus. Jesus then told him, "Feed My sheep," allowing Peter to use the lessons he had learned from his sin to go and sin no more, and to glorify Jesus with his life. Jesus' forgiveness is always greater than anything we can say or do. His ways are unsearchable. His countless thoughts toward us are impossible to comprehend. His grace is immovable. His presence is constant. His vast love for us is immeasurable. His open arms are flung wide. May we all learn to love like that.

CHAPTER 23

"'Therefore say to the house of Israel, "Thus says the Lord GOD: 'I do not do this for your sake, O house of Israel, but for My holy name's sake, which you have profaned among the nations wherever you went. And I will sanctify My great name, which has been profaned among the nations, which you have profaned in their midst; and the nations shall know that I am the LORD,' says the Lord GOD, 'when I am hallowed in you before their eyes. For I will take you from among the nations, gather you out of all countries, and bring you into your own land. Then I will sprinkle clean water on you, and you shall be clean; I will cleanse you from all your filthiness and from all your idols. I will give you a new heart and put a new spirit within you; I will take the heart of stone out of your flesh and give you a heart of flesh. I will put My Spirit within you and cause you to walk in My statutes, and you will keep My judgments and do them. Then you shall dwell in the land that I gave to your fathers; you shall be My people, and I will be your God. I will deliver you from all your uncleannesses. I will call for the grain and multiply it, and bring no famine upon you. And I will multiply the fruit of your trees and the increase of your fields, so that you need never again bear the reproach of famine among the nations. Then you will remember your evil ways and your deeds that were not good; and you will loathe yourselves in your own sight, for your iniquities *and your abominations. Not for your sake do I do* **this**,*' says the Lord GOD, 'let it be known to you. Be ashamed and confounded for your own ways, O house of Israel!' Thus says the Lord GOD: 'On the day that I cleanse you from all your iniquities, I will also enable* **you** *to dwell in the cities, and the ruins shall be rebuilt. The desolate land shall be tilled instead of lying desolate in the sight of all who pass by. So they will say, "This land that was desolate has become like the garden of Eden; and the wasted, desolate, and ruined cities* **are** **now** *fortified* **and** *inhabited." Then the nations which are left all around you shall know that I, the LORD, have rebuilt the ruined places* **and** *planted what was desolate. I the LORD, have spoken* **it**, *and I will do* **it**.*' Thus says the Lord GOD: 'I will also let the house of Israel inquire of Me to do this for them: I will increase their men like a flock. Like a flock* **offered** *as* **holy** *sacrifices, like the flock at Jerusalem on its feast days, so shall the ruined cities be filled with flocks of men. Then they shall know that I* **am** *the LORD.*'"''

~ Ezekiel 36:22-38

By the beginning of the year 2018, God had broken off some pretty big chains in our lives. I was beginning to see and hear Him clearer than ever before and to be able to hear His voice about broader, more general issues that He wanted me to pray for and be involved in—our church, our community, our world—because there was a real healing taking place inside my family. My focus did not have to be so *inward*. I realized at the beginning of 2018 that God was doing so many incredible things in and through our family. Our children were flourishing and growing in the Lord. He was directing them more and more in their areas of gifting and drawing them near to Himself. God was continuing to break down walls in my marriage. Some seen, some unseen.

God spoke to me this year about removing the sacred from the profane, and about not offering food sacrificed to idols. He showed me that so many of our Christian churches and ministries are mixing messages, simply by not guarding their hearts and by adding to or taking away from God's holy Word, thus becoming stumbling blocks to His people. These blurred lines are dangerous, and provide stepping stones for many to fall into the occult and into idol worship.

Our marriage groups have continued, this year studying *Sacred Marriage*[34] by Gary Thomas. Each of these studies has been unique in its focus. The first two centered on us as wives and how we could pray for our husbands and grow in the Lord—individually, and in our marriage relationships. This last study focused more on the marriage relationship as a whole, and how couples are made to worship and glorify God through our marriages. The women in our groups have experienced healing and forgiveness and are being equipped with strength and encouragement to stay in difficult marriages. We broke in June of this year, finishing this study a little early, and God prepared me to finish this book. I am looking forward to connecting with these ladies soon to talk about all God has done in our lives, and to get ready for next year's study.

Journal entry January 8, 2018:

"Ezekiel 36-37

He talks here about His burning jealousy against the rest of the nations, and of taking the heart of stone out of our flesh and leaving a heart of flesh, and about giving us our own land. I think the land He has promised our family is significant not just because it is a promise that will be realized one day, but also a spiritual significance of giving us our own land or territory, as we have been bereaved of it all these years because of our own sin and the captivity resulting from our sin."

Journal entry January 13, 2018:

"Last night, as I was falling asleep, I had a tiny dream (vision?) that sparked me back awake. In the dream, I touched my own arm and it burned me. I was burning as with fire from the inside."

Journal entry January 25, 2018:

"Jeremiah 33:14 '"Behold, the days are coming," says the LORD, "that I will perform that good thing which I have promised to the house of Israel and to the house of Judah."'

Ecclesiastes 3:14 'I know that whatever God does, it shall be forever, nothing can be added to it, and nothing taken from it. God does *it* that men should fear before Him.'"

Journal entry May 25, 2018:

"—And as I write, T is in a Bible study with his men's group from our church. The same men's group he has been attending all these years that he has been back home with us, resulting from the life group which we are still in! GOD is truly amazing! And they are studying *The Screwtape Letters!*"[35]

On June 9, 2018 at a friend's graduation party for their daughter, God introduced me to a dear prophetess (we will call her "Roberta"). Immediately when she met me and shook my hand, she said I was kind and beautiful and patient and that my life was a healing balm, a salve to others. Roberta said that God was going to use all the deep pain He had brought me through to heal others and put a salve on their wounds. She said, "God is using all of your pain and trials and life experiences to strengthen you and enable you to give that strength to others." She said my patience and kindness was like a banana peeling back layers. Roberta also said I had sown many seeds and not seen lots of fruition, but that I would. That the harvest of those seeds sown is coming. She said, "Surely as you have sown in tears, you will reap joy." When she met our daughter, Roberta said I didn't even know what I had there. She said there was something very special about her. She said God was going to do big things. She gave a couple of other words of knowledge about our daughter, and some encouragement to those points, affirming to me that she definitely was hearing this all from the Lord. She said that God was not finished using me and that there was much more to come, and in very powerful ways. She said we were moving forward (my husband and me—I had told her our story briefly at that point) and away from the pain and out into the good, the light—moving forward, moving ahead. Roberta told me to just keep going! She said, "Charge on ahead and don't look back!" This word was from God that day, and I knew it so completely. He knew at this time and for some months by that point, I desperately needed encouragement from Him, as I was being attacked right in my area of gifting on a daily basis. I was so grateful again for that sweet kiss from the Lord. He always knows what we are going through and the strength we need to continue on our path for Him, for His glory.

Journal entry June 12, 2018:

"(Our daughter) woke this morning to the LORD saying her name! I told her to get used to it—He would wake her up all times of the middle of the night to pray."

On June 30 of this year, my family moved from our home in McKinney, where we had lived for fifteen years, to our Celina house. God moved and placed every piece of that puzzle together for HIS glory, right down to the last detail at the last minute. We had waited on Him and had prayed for two years for the vision to come to pass, knowing it had as much or more spiritual significance as it did physical. Through many tears (our daughter and me), we said goodbye to the only home both our children had ever known. God has told me we will have challenges in our new surroundings, but that He has a very specific purpose for us here. We are at His feet and willing to be in His service, whatever the cost. We are grateful for this new chapter in our lives and know that our lives in Him are just beginning. I think we can all say that we are extremely grateful to close the door on the chapter that is behind us.

>Journal entry June 26, 2018:
>
>"Psalm 40
>
>Psalm 41
>
>I am weeping at the thought of leaving this home that we love. I am so grateful for this place, this refuge that He has given my children and me, our family, over all of these years. Peace in the midst of chaos. Calm in the middle of our storm. It has been a beautiful and sweet shelter for our family—in the midst of a storm that is often raging all around us. <u>You</u> are my refuge and my peace, dear Father. You are all we need. I continue to trust You to do what You do best—miracles. <u>You</u> will restore the years the locusts have eaten. You are the GOD of miracles. You are Jehovah Jireh, my Provider, Jehovah Rapha, my Healer, Jehovah Nissi, our Banner who goes before us. Jehovah Shalom, our peace."

The Lord spoke "Celina" to me for several years, prior to specifically imparting His vision for our move. Now that we have moved here, I see the Lord continuing to solidify the vision He gave me. It is a quaint town with a very home-grown feel. There seems to be a real integrity in this people and a comradery here. All through the town there are signs bearing the name. Behind the name is pictured of stalks of wheat, sprouting up in all directions. It is Celina's "symbol." I believe God has shown me this is where we will harvest the wheat that we planted all those years ago, that others may be blessed by its harvest and produce their own fruit for God's kingdom. Our family, as it was, had to die for God to get the glory. "Unless a grain of wheat falls into the ground and dies, it remains alone; but if it dies, it produces much grain" (John 12:24). The time is ripe for harvest.

God took some time to tell me this year that He knows me inside out, and He loves me anyway. He has given me Psalm 139 over and over again. It is truly a beautiful passage in its entirety. The verse that most people recognize from the chapter is verse 14 which says, "I will praise You, for I am fearfully and wonderfully made. Marvelous are Your works, and *that* my soul knows very well." I heard a new song by Tauren Wells the other day entitled, "Known."[36] The chorus sings some profound words for Christians. He writes, "I'm fully known and loved by You. You won't let go no matter what I do. And it's not one or the other; it's hard truth and ridiculous grace—to be fully known and loved by You. I'm fully known and loved by You." If you know Him, friend, then you know His grace. You too, are fully known and fully loved by Him.

Journal entry July 31, 2018:

"Psalm 139 again!

I have seen the most beautiful sunrise this morning, in 68° after many 104-107° days in Texas (we had just returned from vacation), a sweet little Cottontail bunny hopping right out in front of me, a Cardinal flying through the trees, and all kinds of birds singing (Mockingbirds, etc.). I love You, Lord, and Your beautiful creation. Thank You for this day that You have made. I see a Road Runner. I also see the moon setting. Two Road Runners!

Thank You for knowing me inside and out, LORD, when I am misunderstood by just about everyone. Thank You, Lord, for making me and for knowing (and understanding) my innermost thoughts.

Two flocks of birds just flew overhead several minutes apart. The second was just nesting in the tops of these nearby trees! I didn't see them at all until they flew out."

On August 3, a friend invited me to an impromptu night of worship at our church taking place the following evening. My husband was out of town, and I realized the next day that both my children would be gone for different events. I had to drop our daughter at the church for a youth event, so I decided to attend. That evening as we worshipped in the theater of our church, God spoke so much truth to me. He gave me many different pictures for my family and for me, several of which I am still pondering with Him. I saw myself driving down the long, country road to our new home, worshipping Him. I saw myself just sitting with Him on our front porch, reading His Word. Finally, I saw myself walking around my house, singing and worshipping Him. I drove home and had a restful evening in the Lord. The next morning when I awoke, I knew God wanted me to do the things He had shown me. After sitting with the Lord in His Word for a while, I turned on some worship music by Bethel and began anointing my home with songs. I sang my heart out to the Lord in every room of our new home, pausing to pray as He led in our bedroom and the children's bedrooms and a couple of other rooms. This was my love offering to Him. All told, I had a 24-hour rest and worship intensive with God.

Journal entry August 4, 2018:

"I have just been in my home for three hours listening to worship music, reading His Word, and singing and worshipping while listening to Bethel all over our house. Every room has now been anointed and bathed in worship, concentrating on our children's bedrooms, the piano room, (our daughter's) music room in the attic loft, the family room, and lastly our bedroom.

Beautiful Day, LORD.

Catherine E. Brock

Isaiah 27-28"

The very next evening, after all of my family was home together again, our son was burned very badly in a brush fire outside our home. We rushed him to the small emergency room in Prosper that night—then they ambulanced him to Parkland Hospital, downtown Dallas. He had second-degree burns all over the right side of his face, his neck, and all down his right arm and hand. This was the third time in his fifteen, almost sixteen years, that the enemy had tried to take his life—one other time with his appendix bursting, and once with a bad staph infection in his ankle, hospitalized for five days each time. The Lord had shown me back then, and He reminded me during this crisis, that this boy had a very high calling on his life. The enemy wanted to take him; but God said NO. God also reminded me a few days after this current incident, that He had prepared my heart and my home with worship. Our home was dedicated to Him. He knew all of this was coming; and He prepared my heart with a restful and peaceful posture of worship to my King.

Three weekends later, our daughter and I had a weekend alone at our home to go through Dr. James Dobson's *Preparing for Adolescence*,[37] a similar tool to *Passport to Purity* that we used with our son four years before. This particular weekend, our boys were away on a bonding trip in Oklahoma that we had given my husband for Father's Day. Thankfully by this point, our son was beginning to heal and was cleared by the Parkland Burn Clinic to do normal activities, with the prerequisite that he lathered himself in sunscreen and stayed out of the sun in general while he was healing. On the Saturday of the purity weekend with our daughter, the exercise that went along with the lesson was for her to write down things that she didn't like (or even hated) about herself. She was then to put checkmarks by the things that bothered her the most, prioritizing these as her focus. Next, she was to talk to someone she was close to (me) and let that person speak words of life over her, finding solutions for the things that could change, and bringing wisdom to be able to see the other things in a different light if at all possible—while understanding that there were some things which would not change. Finally, she and I were to take that list and give it to God, asking Him to heal the wounds in her heart and to help her to accept things that would not change, then burn the list. We did so, in the burn bin in our backyard, the exact spot where the enemy had tried to take our son's life exactly 21 days before. God was re-claiming HIS territory for this family. We were and surely are HIS own.

On the night of August 30, 2018, I had a revelation from God. I was going to bed when God startled me awake with the realization that our entire marriage—and my position in our marriage—was a complete spiritual posturing. God had called me to love my husband as Hosea loved the prostitute, just like He told me to pray to do several years ago. He has placed us here as a message of His love for so many, and as an example of how to love like He does. God, may we love each other more faithfully, and always unto YOU.

The weekend of October 5-7 was a truly spiritually significant weekend. God allowed me to lead worship for our daughter's "Savior Seekers" mother/daughter backyard campout. I loved listening to all the beautiful voices of these girls and their mamas worshipping the Lord together. It was truly heavenly. The next night we had those same girls (and a couple more!) at our home for our daughter's 12th birthday slumber party. Thankfully, they were all exhausted and in bed by 12:30! Our sweet daughter thanked me so many times that night for making her party a huge success. As exhausted as I was, I was so thankful God had helped me push all the way through that weekend. The next day she hugged me tightly, and told me (still not letting go) that I was in a <u>race</u>, reminding me that she had already told me this before, and that the end would definitely be better than the beginning—that we would have a triumphant end. I told her she had truly spoken a prophetic word from the LORD, and one that I <u>greatly</u> needed to hear! I prayed with her then and there that only the <u>truth</u> of Jesus Christ would ever take root in her heart and in her brother's heart—and that all the lies of the enemy would fall away.

Three weeks later, we celebrated our son's birthday by hosting our fourth annual camping trip with his friends. This time was by far the most congruent, the most harmonious trip we have made—even including our early exit the second night due to a downpour of rain! The boys all just bunked upstairs the second night and had a glorious time.

Seven years ago, our son had the dream of our family back in our home together, talking of putting in a pool right before his birthday. God was giving us His hope for the future back then, a hope for things to come.

Catherine E. Brock

This year it came to pass. We were putting in a pool, right before our son's sixteenth birthday. The pool was completed as I wrote this today, three weeks after his birthday. I can't wait to see the goodness our Lord has in store for us.

CHAPTER 24

"Sing, O heavens, for the Lord has done it! Shout, you lower parts of the earth; break forth into singing, you mountains, o forest and every tree in it! For the LORD has redeemed Jacob, and glorified Himself in Israel."

~ Isaiah 44:23

My family is certainly not perfect in any regard, or by any stretch of *anyone's* imagination. But we are healing. We have been redeemed. God allowed me to see the blessing of my father repenting to my mother and asking her forgiveness on her deathbed. My grandmother even forgave my father and gave up years of bitterness on that day. Years later, I now have an excellent relationship with my stepfather, whom I call "Dad" as well as my own dad. We even have a day that commemorates his adopting me, which we call "Name Day." I have a sweet relationship with my brother who is his son, and my brother's wife and family. They love the Lord and are charging ahead for him. My father and I have a wonderful relationship. I lovingly call him, "my little Daddy." He has seen my highs and lows and has been my champion through it all. I love him dearly, and also his wife whom I endearingly call "Mama Sue." I have good relationships with my sisters and brother who came from this union as well. God even allowed me to have a loving relationship with the woman my stepfather married after my mom died. Many years before her death in 2017, we became good friends; and I know she prayed fervently for my family. God has also brought much healing to my relationship with my husband's entire family. I love them all, and I know they have my back.

My heart-friend Janice's husband is home with their family now—He came home in 2012, several months before my husband did. Their family, like mine, has been watching God work miracles for a very long time.

Several years ago, God made a way for me to make amends to my first husband. He was very forgiving when I asked, and also asked my forgiveness for his sin. I am so truly grateful to God for this healing.

God did what He promised us He would do. He made my husband and I and each of our children a promise of healing and restoration, and He delivered. He made good on His promise. God always keeps His promises. Isaiah 45:23 declares, "I have sworn by Myself; the word has gone out of My mouth *in* righteousness, and shall not return, that to Me every knee shall bow, every tongue shall take an oath." He is faithful. He *will* do it. He will bring it to pass.

God wants us to have an ongoing, two-way relationship with Him. He invites us in Jeremiah 33:3 by saying, "Call to Me, and I will answer you, and show you great and mighty things, which you do not know." (God actually used the entire chapter of Jeremiah 33 to encourage me greatly while my husband and I were separated.) If we are His children, and we have Jesus living in our hearts as our Savior, He says in I John 5:14, "Now this is the confidence that we have in Him, that if we ask anything according to His will, He hears us. And if we know that He hears us, whatever we ask, we know that we have the petitions that we have asked of Him." Last time I checked, *anything* means *anything*. He is our Abba Father, our big Daddy, our Comforter, our Shield, our Protector, our Rear Guard. He watches us in the night and in the *night seasons* when it feels like no one else knows we are there, or cares. He's always got our back. He can't wait to rescue us. We just have to *ask Him*. And so often He rescues us and protects us from things we didn't even know were there or a danger to us. But He wants us to communicate with Him. Because He loves us. He loves you more than you could ever know. He loves you with all of His heart.

Jeremiah 31 talks of how the Lord loves us. He writes in His love letter, the Bible, to us, "The LORD has appeared of old to me, *saying*: 'Yes, I have loved you with an everlasting love; therefore with lovingkindness I have drawn you. Again I will build you, and you shall be rebuilt, o virgin Israel! You shall be adorned with your tambourines, and shall go forth in the dances of those who rejoice. You shall yet plant vines on the mountains of Samaria; the planters shall plant and eat *them* as ordinary food. For there shall be a day *when* the watchmen will cry on Mount Ephraim, "Arise, and let us go up to Zion, to the LORD, our God."'" (Jeremiah 31:3-6).

Also in verse 12, He talks of our rejoicing in Him! He says, "Therefore they shall come and sing in the height of Zion, streaming to the goodness of the LORD—for wheat and new wine and oil, for the young of the flock and the herd; their souls shall be like a well-watered garden, and they shall sorrow no more at all." The entirety of that chapter is excellent and encouraging for families, and for all of the family of God. I recommend digging in deeper with Him!

There is a song that I love by Kari Jobe, called "Beautiful."[38] The lyrics say, "Here, in Your presence, I am not afraid of brokenness. To wash your feet with humble tears, I would be poured out till nothing's left." This is how He wants us to come to Him. Broken, humble, unafraid, unashamed because of His love for us poured out on the cross. He gave all for us. He wants us to love Him with our lives in return. Matthew 9:16-17 says (Jesus speaking), "No one puts a piece of unshrunk cloth on an old garment, for the patch pulls away from the garment and the tear is made worse. Nor do they put new wine into old wineskins, or else the wineskins break, the wine is spilled, and the wineskins are ruined. But they put new wine into new wineskins, and both are preserved." Jesus wants to heal us so that He can use us for His kingdom, for His glory. He wants to be able to pour the new wine into the new wineskins. But first, we have to take all our mess to Him and let Him clean us up.

Sometimes the journey seems long and hard and, well, just too much to bear. God will give us strength for the battle, every time. He tells us throughout the first book of Joshua to be strong and courageous! And then He arms us with His strength, and with the strength of His Word. Joshua 1:7-9 states, "'Only be strong and very courageous, that you may observe to do according to all the law which Moses My servant commanded you; do not turn from it to the right hand or to the left, that you may prosper wherever you go. This book of the Law shall not depart from your mouth, but you shall meditate in it day and night, that you may observe to do according to all that is written in it. For then you will make your way prosperous, and then you will have good success. Have I not commanded you? Be strong and of good courage; do not be afraid, nor be dismayed, for the LORD your God *is* with you wherever you go.'" Verse 18 reiterates, "Only be strong and of good courage."

Think God is trying to get a point across?? He's got us! We are not to fear because we have the LORD on our side!!! HIS strength is enough to carry us through whatever we may be facing at whatever point or time in our lives. He is always aware, always watching, never sleeping, always caring, always carrying us. And HE WILL deliver us. We just have to trust Him. Joshua 1:3 gives us a very encouraging promise, "'Every place that the sole of your foot will tread upon I have given you.'" God was making this promise to Joshua, directly after Moses had died, as He passed the baton to Joshua to lead the Israelites to conquer and take over the Promised Land that He was giving them. He would not fail them. They just had to *trust* Him.

He will not fail you, either. Joshua, in turn, encouraged his followers with a word from the Lord. We see this in verse 13, "'Remember the word which Moses the servant of the LORD commanded you, saying, "The LORD your God is giving you rest and is giving you this land."'"

When God allows your path to cross with the weary, remember to point them to God. He wants to use your life to encourage others in their walk with Him, so that He continues to get all the glory, no matter what! He will be faithful to carry their load as well.

Finally, Joshua 21:43-45 states, "So the LORD gave to Israel all the land of which He had sworn to give to their fathers, and they took possession of it and dwelt in it. The LORD gave them rest all around, according to all that He had sworn to their fathers. And not a man of all their enemies stood against them; the LORD delivered all their enemies into their hand. Not a word failed of any good thing which the LORD had spoken to the house of Israel. All came to pass."

God keeps His promises to His children. He loves to do that. It's just who He is.

You can trust Him with your very life.

What is He promising you today?

AFTER THOUGHTS

Jesus will give us an abundant life if we will <u>*surrender*</u> to Him. All that we are, all that we have. All our hopes and dreams. All our pride. He will give us *His* dreams—and His are better than ours ever could be. And they will come true, if we surrender all. If we let Him work at our point of failure. It's not too late. His utmost desire for us is victory. He is not going to gloss over our failures or say something trite about our losses. He is going to pick us up and show us how to do it His way. Victoriously. No matter how many times we fall. He is our Champion. He is our KING.

> *"And let us not grow weary while doing good, for in due season we shall reap if we do not lose heart."*
>
> *~ Galatians 6:9*

END NOTES AND ENCOURAGEMENT

1. Bowles, Heloise. "Hints from Heloise." Honolulu Advertiser/King Features Syndicate 1959-1977.
2. *The Waltons*. CBS. Lorimar Productions, Warner Bros. Domestic Television Distribution. 14 Sep. 1972 – 4 June 1981. Television.
3. King, Carol. "It's Too Late." *Tapestry,* Ode, 1971, track 3.
4. *Sesame Street*. PBS. Children's Television Workshop/Sesame Workshop. 1993 – present. Television.
5. *The Electric Company*. PBS. Children's Television Workshop/Sesame Workshop. 25 Oct. 1971 – 15 April 1977. Television.
6. Pearl, Debi. *Created to be His Help Meet*, 10th ann. rev. exp. ed. (Pleasantville: No Greater Joy Ministries Inc., 2014).
7. Eldredge, John and Stasi. *Captivating* (Nashville: Thomas Nelson, 2010).
8. Chambers, Oswald. *My Uttmost for His Highest* (Uhrichsville: Barbour Publishing, Inc., 1935).
9. Patillo, Leon. "Flesh of My Flesh." *Don't Give In*, Word Music, LLC, 2009, track 3.
10. *Facing the Giants*. Dir. Alex Kendrick. Sherwood Pictures, 2006.
11. Lucado, Max. *Facing Your Giants* (Nashville: Thomas Nelson, 2006).
12. *The Lion, the Witch, and the Wardrobe*. Dir. Andrew Adamson. Walt Disney Pictures; Walden Media, 2005.
13. Miller, J.P. *The Little Red Hen* (New York: Little Golden Book/Penguin Random House, 2001).
14. *Fireproof*. Dir. Alex Kendrick. Sherwood Pictures, 2008.
15. Kendrick, Alex and Stephen. *The Love Dare* (Nashville: B & H Publishing Group, 2008).
16. Keller, Tim. *The Prodigal God* (New York: Penguin Random House, 2011).
17. Blackaby, Henry T. and Claude V. King. *Experiencing God* (Nashville: Broadman & Holman Publishers, 1994).
18. Hillman, Os. "Affirming New Leadership." Today God is First (TGIF) 13 September, 2011, http://www.TodayGodIsFirst.com.
19. Eggerichs, Emerson. *Love & Respect* (Nashville: Thomas Nelson, 2004).

20 Arterburn, Stephen and Fred Stoeker. *Every Man's Battle* (Colorado Springs: Waterbrook Press, 2002).
21 Harley, Willard F. Jr. *His Needs, Her Needs* (Grand Rapids: Revell, 2011).
22 Catt, Michael and Stephen and Alex Kendrick. *Courageous* (Nashville: Lifeway, 2012).
23 *Weekend to Remember*®, a ministry of Family Life®, Dennis Rainey and Bob Lepine co-founders. http://www.familylifetoday.com/program/weekend-to-remember-wonderful.
24 Cloud, Henry and John Townsend. *Boundaries* (Grand Rapids: Zondervan, 1992).
25 Moore, Beth. *Sacred Secrets* (Nashville: Lifeway, 2013).
26 Rainey, Dennis and Barbara. *Passport to Purity* (Little Rock: Family Life, 2018).
27 Dobson, James C. *The Strong-Willed Child* (Carol Stream: Tyndale, 1978).
28 Dobson, James C. *The New Strong-Willed Child* (Wheaton: Tyndale, 2004).
29 Leonard, David and Leslie Jordan, All Sons and Daughters. "All the Poor and Powerless." *Brokenness Aside,* Integrity's Alleluia! Music, Integrity's Praise! Music/Capitol CMG Publishing, 2011, track 3.
30 Duewel, Wesley L. "You Must Use the Command of Faith." *Touch the World through Prayer* (Grand Rapids: Zondervan,1986).
31 Omartian, Stormie. *The Power of a Praying Wife* (Eugene: Harvest House Publishers, 2014).
32 EvangeCube® International, 317 Main St., #207, Franklin, TN 37064.
33 Qureshi, Nabeel. *Seeking Allah, Finding Jesus* (Grand Rapids, Zondervan, 2016).
34 Thomas, Gary. *Sacred Marriage* (Grand Rapids: Zondervan, 2000).
35 Lewis, C.S. *The Screwtape Letters* (New York: Simon & Schuster, 1996).
36 Wells, Tauren. "Known." *Hills and Valleys (Deluxe Edition),* Reunion, 2018, track 6.
37 Dobson, James C. *Preparing for Adolescence* (Colorado Springs: Focus on the Family, 1999).
38 Jobe, Kari. "Beautiful." *Kari Jobe,* Gateway Music, 2010, track 5.
39 Gretzinger, Steffany Frizzell and Bethel Music. "We Dance." *You Make Me Brave: Live at the Civic,* Bethel Music Publishing, 2013, track 9.
40 David, Jonathan and Melissa Helser and Bethel Music. "No Longer Slaves (Live)." *We Will Not Be Shaken (Live),* Bethel Music Publishing, 2015, track 4.
41 Asbury, Cory. "Reckless Love." *Reckless Love*, Bethel Music, 2018, track 1.
42 Williams, Zach. "Fear is a Liar." *Chainbreaker (Deluxe Edition),* Provident Label Group, Sony Music Entertainment, 2016, track 8.
43 Springer, Rita. "Defender." *Battles,* Chris Greely and Eric Lemiere, 2017, track 4.
44 Johnson, Brian and Bethel Music. "We Will Not Be Shaken (Live)." *We Will Not Be Shaken (Live),* Bethel Music Publishing, 2015, track 1.

"PEACE" VERSES

1. Numbers 6:26 "'The Lord bless you and keep you; the LORD make His face shine upon you, and be gracious to you; the LORD lift up His countenance upon you, and give you peace.'"
2. Psalm 4:8 "I will both lie down in peace, and sleep; for You alone, O LORD, make me dwell in safety."
3. Psalm 142:6-7 "Pray for the peace of Jerusalem: 'may they prosper who love you. Peace be within your walls, prosperity within your palaces.' For the sake of my brethren and companions, I will now say, Peace *be* within you.' Because of the house of the LORD our God I will seek your good."
4. Isaiah 26:3 "You will keep *him* in perfect peace, *whose* mind is stayed on *You*, because he trusts in You. Trust in the LORD forever, for in YAH, the LORD, *is* everlasting strength."
5. John 16:33 "'These things I have spoken to you, that in Me you may have peace. In the world you will have tribulation; but be of good cheer, I have overcome the world.'"

"JOY" VERSES

1. Nehemiah 8:10 "'Do not sorrow, for the joy of the LORD is your strength.'"
2. Psalm 30:5 "For His anger *is but for* a moment, His favor *is for* life; weeping may endure for a night, but joy *comes* in the morning."
3. Galatians 5:22-23 "But the fruit of the Spirit is love, joy, peace, longsuffering, kindness, goodness, faithfulness, gentleness, self-control. Against such there is no law."
4. John 15:11 "'These things I have spoken to you, that My joy may remain in you, and *that* your joy may be full.'"
5. James 1:2-4 "My brethren, count it all joy when you fall into various trials, knowing that the testing of your faith produces patience. But let patience have *its* perfect work, that you may be perfect and complete, lacking nothing."

"The wilderness and the wasteland shall be glad for them,
And the desert shall rejoice and blossom as the rose;
It shall blossom abundantly and rejoice,
Even with joy and singing.
The glory of Lebanon shall be given to it,
The excellence of Carmel and Sharon.
They shall see the glory of the LORD,
The excellency of our God.
Strengthen the weak hands,
And make firm the feeble knees.
Say to those who are fearful-hearted,
'Be strong, do not fear!
Behold your God will come with vengeance,
With the recompense of God;
He will come and save you.'
Then the eyes of the blind shall be opened,
And the ears of the deaf shall be unstopped.
Then the lame shall leap like a deer,
And the tongue of the dumb sing.
For waters shall burst forth in the wilderness,
And streams in the desert.
The parched ground shall become a pool,
And the thirsty land springs of water;
In the habitation of jackals where each lay,
There shall be grass with reeds and rushes.
A highway shall be there, and a road,
And it shall be called the Highway of Holiness.
The unclean shall not pass over it,
But it shall be for others.
Whoever walks the road, although a fool,
Shall not go astray.
No lion shall be there,
Nor shall any ravenous beast go up on it;
It shall not be found there.
But the redeemed shall walk there,
And the ransomed of the LORD shall return,
And come to Zion with singing,
With everlasting joy on their heads.
They shall obtain joy and gladness,
And sorrow and sighing shall flee away." ~ **Isaiah 35**

"'…Because the LORD has been
 witness
Between you and the wife of your
 youth,
With whom you have dealt
 treacherously;
Yet she is your companion
And your wife by covenant.
But did He not make them one,
Having a remnant of the Spirit?
And why one?
He seeks godly offspring.
Therefore take heed to your spirit,
And let none deal treacherously
 with the wife of his youth.

For the LORD God of Israel says
That He hates divorce,
For it covers one's garment with
 violence,'
Says the LORD of hosts,
'Therefore take heed to your spirit
That you do not deal
 treacherously.'" ~ **Malachi 2:14-16**

"'And I will rebuke the devourer
 for your sakes,
So that he will not destroy the fruit
 of your ground,
Nor shall the vine fail to bear fruit
 for you in the field.'
Says the LORD of hosts;
'And all nations will call you
 blessed,
For you will be a delightful
 land,'
Says the LORD of hosts." ~ **Malachi 3:11-12**

GRATITUDE

Thank You, God, for placing me on this project and for holding my hand every step of the way. Thank You for teaching me who I truly am in You - and for never letting go of my hand. You are my everything.

I thank my husband and my children for your patience as I finished the work the Lord gave me to do. I could not have done this without your love and support. You're all my favorites! I love you to the moon and back.

Thank you, Mama L, for loving me like a daughter all of these years. Your wisdom is priceless. You are truly my gift from God.

Thank you, Jennifer Clark, for your steadfast heart, listening ear, godly advice, prayers and never-ending friendship. I wouldn't have made it through without you.

Thank you, Patti Davidson, for the picture of Jesus you are to me and to a watching world. Thank you and Ron for your constant prayers for my family and me. Thank you for loving me, no matter what. Everyone should have a "Bunny!"

Thank you, Lali Stanley (and Niji Stanley!), for warring for us in the heavenlies. Thank you also for making me laugh when I need it most. You are a beautiful wife, mama and friend.

Thank you, Terri Earls, for being a kindred spirit and a true example of a wife and mother (of six!) to me. You make it all look so easy. Thank you and Jason for your constant prayers and for always listening to God's heart.

Thank you, Novelette Collins, for going the extra mile to show me that you love me. Thank you for being God's mouthpiece, and for not being afraid to speak the truth. I am so grateful for our Collins clan!

Thank you, Nicole (Cinderelly) Raphiel, for always being in my corner. I will never forget the day we met. You are one special lady. I love you and your crew.

Thank you, Heather Simpson, for your friendship, advice on marriage and just general godly wisdom. You are a wealth of knowledge!

Thank you, Edna Pajela, for your prayers for my family, your love for my boy (and my girl) and for the twenty-second hug. It has made *all* the difference.

Thank you, Teri Simpson, for your friendship, wisdom, peace, encouragement and your Jesus-loving heart. Thank you for *always* pointing me to Him.

I thank my sisters in our marriage-intensive groups. Without your support and encouragement, I would have crashed a long time ago!

Thank you, Julie Earl, for being fearless in the ministry God has given you. Thank you also for your help in editing this book! Your life is a shining example of Christ.

Thank you, Bethany Anderson, for being my prayer partner, encourager, and general inspiration in writing this book! You gave me the push to go ahead. I am grateful for our friendship!

Thank you, Ramona Walden, for your giving heart. Your example of stewardship is priceless.

Thank you, Darla Melton, for always speaking your heart and never being afraid to tell me how you really feel. I love you for your honesty. You are helping many with your testimony of God's truth in your life.

Thank you, Missy Staben, for rescuing me from disaster more than once, and for always being on my side.

Thank you, Joy Prather, for the example of patience, grace and love that you set with your life. I am indebted to you for your hours of listening.

Thank you, my Maria, our "Aunt Ria," for never giving up on me and for loving me through thick and thin. God surely knew what He was doing when He placed you in my life all of those years ago!

I thank my dad and Mama Sue, my stepdad ("Dad") and my brothers and sisters who have prayed and believed for our marriage. Your prayers were heard and answered. I love you all with my life. I am so very grateful for you.

I thank my mama for being my biggest advocate on the planet. And for loving me with her very life.

ABOUT THE AUTHOR

Catherine E. Brock is a wife, mama, daughter, sister, friend and Jesus lover. She loves to sing and worship the Lord, be crazy with her hubby and kids, and has a passion for marriage ministry and mentoring women. Catherine currently resides in Celina, Texas with her husband, son, daughter, Molli (Boxer) and Emma (Yorkshire Terrier). *Unveiled* is her first book and is an outpouring of the love of the Holy Spirit from an obedient heart.

Lightning Source UK Ltd.
Milton Keynes UK
UKHW020313310819
348844UK00003B/759/P